MORE THAN PETTICOATS

Remarkable KENTUCKY WOMEN

MORE THAN PETTICOATS

Remarkable KENTUCKY WOMEN

Mimi O'Malley

gpp

Guilford, Connecticut

To my family: Mike, John, Kate, Anne Bourdet, Andre Bourdet, Emily Bourdet, Bob O'Malley, and Marie O'Malley

Layout: Sue Murray
Project editors: Ellen Urban & Meredith Dias

Library of Congress Cataloging-in-Publication Data is available on file.

ISBN 978-0-7627-6148-7

Printed in the United States of America

10 9 8 7 6 5 4 3 2 1

CONTENTS

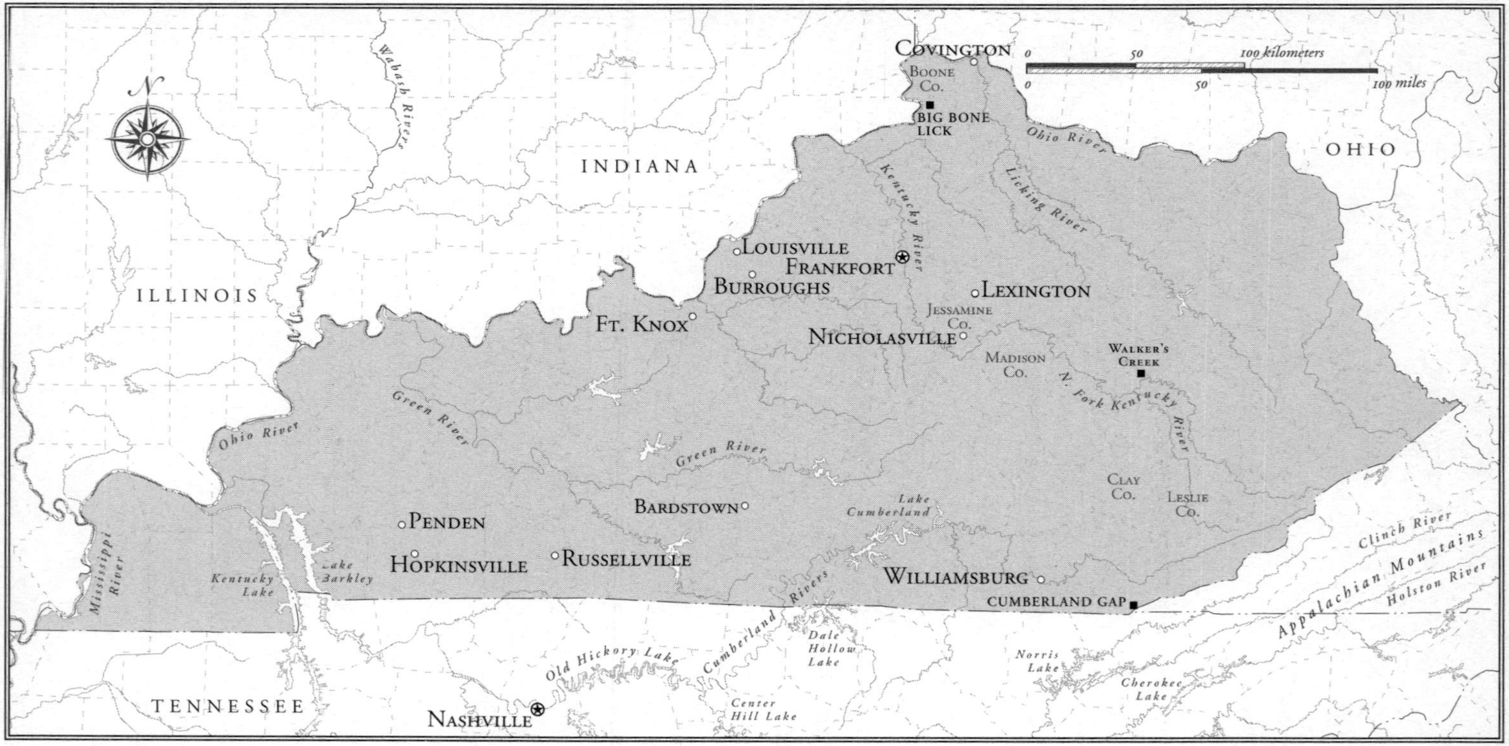

COVINGTON
BOONE CO.
BIG BONE LICK
0 50 100 kilometers
0 50 100 miles
Ohio River
OHIO
INDIANA
ILLINOIS
N
Wabash Rivers
Kentucky River
Licking River
LOUISVILLE
FRANKFORT
BURROUGHS
LEXINGTON
JESSAMINE CO.
NICHOLASVILLE
FT. KNOX
MADISON CO.
WALKER'S CREEK
N. Fork Kentucky River
Green River
Ohio River
BARDSTOWN
Lake Cumberland
CLAY CO.
LESLIE CO.
PENDEN
HOPKINSVILLE
RUSSELLVILLE
WILLIAMSBURG
CUMBERLAND GAP
Mississippi River
Kentucky Lake
Lake Barkley
Cumberland Rivers
Clinch River
Appalachian Mountains
Holston River
Old Hickory Lake
Dale Hollow Lake
Norris Lake
Cherokee Lake
Center Hill Lake
TENNESSEE
NASHVILLE

KENTUCKY

ACKNOWLEDGMENTS

The author gratefully acknowledges the assistance of David Coleman, Fort Harrod State Park; Anna Powell, Sisters of Charity of Nazareth; Jennifer DuPlaga and Liz Thompson, Kentucky Historical Society; Jason Flahardy, University of Kentucky Archives; Nathalie Andrews, Portland Museum; Amy Purcell, University of Louisville Special Collections; Amy Inskeep, *Louisville Courier Journal;* Charles House, Clay County Genealogical and Historical Society; Robert Henry; Amy Wallace, the Filson Historical Society; Dr. Kathleen Bean, University of Louisville School of Law; and Liz Chase, Emory University Special Collections. The author would like to extend much gratitude to Rachel Howard, University of Louisville; Virginia Mattingly, University of Louisville School of Law; Krystle Feathers and Sara Ekart of The Learning House, Inc., for their patience and expertise on digital technology and intellectual property.

INTRODUCTION

It's been more than ten years since a book on notable Kentucky women has been published. Eugenia Potter's *Kentucky Women: Two Centuries of Indomitable Spirit and Vision* beautifully captures the profiles of Kentucky women and was an inspiration for this book. Carol Crowe-Carraco's *Women Who Made a Difference* highlights a few Kentucky female notables for younger readers. However, it was time to review what researchers have uncovered about our favorite Kentucky women as well as highlight some new ladies who haven't received the recognition they so rightly deserve.

Kentucky state history is known for its prominent men including Captain Thomas Walker, Daniel Boone, Henry Clay, Abraham Lincoln, Louis Brandeis, and Robert Bingham. Kentucky has also put forth a number of women who've played a viable role in both state and national history. The idea to concentrate on women seems to be a natural spin-off of my other title, *It Happened in Kentucky,* which highlights interesting events that helped define Kentucky's rich history. While researching that book, the stories that had the greatest appeal were those of Jenny Wiley, Jane Crawford, Delia Webster, and Carol Sutton. These ladies are just a small fraction of Kentucky's finest.

I hope you enjoy reading *More Than Petticoats: Remarkable Kentucky Women,* which chronicles Kentucky women whose contributions shaped not only Kentucky state history but US history. Every attempt was made to represent Kentucky women from all over the commonwealth as well as a variety of subject areas, including law, military science, journalism, fine arts, transportation, education, medicine, sociology, and music. Although all but one of these women were born prior to the twentieth century, their influence has been felt all the way into the twenty-first century. Hopefully, these ladies' biographies will inspire readers well into the next millennium.

Jane Coomes

(1750–1816)

KENTUCKY'S FIRST SCHOOLTEACHER

The party was exhausted after its trek across the Wilderness Trail, which originated in Maryland and extended through southeastern Virginia and Tennessee and across present-day eastern Kentucky. Only twenty-five years earlier, parts of this trail were explored by Captain Thomas Walker and his Loyal Land Company expedition. In this expedition William Coomes and his party were ready to encamp and begin a hunting expedition to feed their hungry contingency at Drennon's Lick, near present-day Frankfort. Coomes was accompanied on this excursion by Dr. George Hart and Abraham and Isaac Hite, the first Catholics to set foot in Kentucky.

Also accompanying Coomes was his wife, Jane Coomes, who organized a small group not involved in the hunting expedition to collect a few kettles and begin boiling salt from the nearby spring. The task was no simple chore, for it could take eight hundred to one thousand gallons of salty spring water and several days of stoking coals under the hot fire to produce one bushel of salt. A half-pint of salt marked an entire day of work. This allotment was the equivalent of one British pound (about $137 today), a good cow and calf, or one thousand pounds of tobacco.

The Cherokee, Shawnee, and Chickasaw tribes, the three largest tribes inhabiting the region, were proficient in the art of boiling salt, but the early settlers lacked not only the materials but the manpower needed to undertake salt boiling on a regular basis. In fact, salt boiling was a dangerous task since the three salt springs known to early Kentucky settlers—Bullitt's Lick on the Salt River, Blue Licks on the Licking, and Drennon's Lick on the Kentucky—resided within Cherokee, Shawnee, and Chickasaw hunting territory and were prone to attack. A vigilant eye was necessary to ensure the safety of salt camps. This was not easy since the kettles were suspended on chains from a forked pyramid above an open fire. Certainly the fire alone would have raised a red flag that someone was nearby. No stranger to danger, Jane Coomes's salt-making party, the first recorded for a white female settler within Kentucky, did its best to disguise its whereabouts.

These settlers were accustomed to making salt as regularly as fetching water, growing crops, and hunting wild game. The colonists used three types of salt: bay salt from the ocean, white salt boiled out of rock impurities, and rock or mineral salt found in the earth. Back east every town or city had a salt blockhouse or "bay" saltworks that employed local townspeople to manufacture salt using gigantic vats to dilute sea salt. Rumor of plentiful salt came from former captives of Indians who ventured from the West to the East, stirring interest in prospective salt entrepreneurs to head west. Moreover, salt became a tax commodity for the British to use against wayward colonists.

Salt was the preferred method for preserving meat since salt delays the breaking down and decomposition of meat, ensuring a longer shelf life. After animal hides dried out, salt was added to absorb the water from the albumen. Salt was also used as a means of trade. Fur, flour, tobacco, whiskey, hemp, and yarn were a few items bartered for salt. Pioneers also used salt for cowlicks, tanning hides, and for medical purposes such as antiseptics. It was common for settlers to travel long distances to secure salt, so the ability to procure salt nearby was an asset to building a pioneer life. The Ohio River fed many springs, creeks, and streams. Sandstone that overlies slate seems to furnish salt springs, which in some areas could be reached anywhere between three hundred to five hundred feet below the ground.

Yet Jane Coomes's prominence extends beyond being the first Kentucky settler to attempt salt making. As one of the first Catholic families

Replica of the interior of Kentucky's first schoolhouse, where Jane Coombs presided Old Fort Harrod State Park, Harrodsburg, KY

to emigrate from Charles County, Maryland, Jane and her husband, William, were part of Abraham Hite's surveying expedition in 1775. The Coomes family ventured across Wilderness Road, eventually reaching Fort Harrod on September 8, 1775. Fort Harrod was one of three permanent settlements developed by prospector James Harrod the previous summer (the other two were Logan's Station and Boonesborough). It resided about one mile from the Salt River on a large spring.

Construction of a stockade started in the fall of 1775, complete with puncheon walls made from heavy timbers set on end and close together. Cabins twenty feet square lined the inside of the stockade. Cabin floors consisted of wood plank or dirt, and chimneys were made from stone, straw, and mud. Cabin windows were a rarity and of the few that did exist, none had glass. Residing at all four corners of the fort, blockhouses extended three to four feet above the stockade walls with rifle portholes for protection and surveillance. The fort enclosed an area of an acre and a half, with a spring and a stream running through it. In the center was a powder magazine. Although constructing Fort Harrod demanded physical brawn and tremendous manpower, a certain mathematical and analytical acumen was needed to survey half-acre in-lots, ten-acre out-lots, and road construction.

By the time the Coomes family arrived, the settlement had been victim to sporadic Indian attacks, scaring half of the settlers to flee back east. No sooner would a group of settlers leave than another would take their place. In their wake the water supply around the fort became polluted. Animal waste littered what little space was available in and around the immediate area of the compound. Two years after construction Fort Harrod housed 198 people—10 percent were slaves, 35 percent were white children, and 12 percent were white women. The compactness of the area was further compounded by seasonal elements of spring mud, summer insects, and winter ice. Those who entered Fort Harrod's gates included a who's who of Kentucky notables: George Rogers Clark, an Episcopal priest and first minister in Kentucky Reverend John Lythe, Coomes, Hart, and the Hite men. Living in the fort firmed one's resolve to move away from it as soon as one could fortify the area around it.

The typical settler had limited formal schooling, and those who were educated were products of private academies in Virginia or Maryland rather than public schools. Private academies were supported by individuals who sought occupations as lawyers, doctors, ministers, teachers, merchants, land surveyors, and the like. Many private academies were funded by religious sects or functioned as prep schools for colleges, but most, if not all, were sustained without taxation. The Land Ordinance of 1785, which designated a specific proportion of public lands for educational use, actually did little to finance the founding and support of schools. But it served to plant the idea of the public school in the mind of the frontiersman.

At the urging of the fort's residents, Jane Coomes was charged with the task of opening a school to educate the children living in the fort. By fall 1777, records showed that one-third of Fort Harrod's residents were under the age of ten. The first classroom consisted of a room built of round logs with no chinking in between that sat alongside the fort. The floor was made of dirt, and there was one window, which was covered with doeskin instead of glass, and a slab door hung on deer throngs. Seats were made from puncheons or logs cut lengthwise, with no backs. Among Jane Coomes's pupils were her own children and those from the families of Harrodstown founders such as Thomas Denton, Richard Hogan, and Hugh McGary. Jane Coomes taught her students to read and write from paddle-shaped pine shingles. These shingles were inscribed with the alphabet, numbers, and simple prayers. Shingles doubled as a source of punishment if students warranted it. The Dillard's Speller and the New Testament readings were the only required texts.

Dame schools like Jane Coomes's originated in England in the fifteenth century, with the core focus of educating children in small towns or rural areas in elementary curriculum. Dubbed by the "dames who picked up children at their parents' door," dame schools were a precursor to preschools that provided a general education curriculum prior to younger students moving to either a public or private school. Compared to classes of today, teaching methods in dame schools consisted of basic rote memorization. In this "blab school," as it was dubbed, it was common to hear students study out loud as part of Coomes's instructional technique of the day. New Testament text took the place of the hornbooks prevalent in eighteenth-century England. Any pay Coomes received was in the form of tobacco, bacon, or bear meat.

Coomes taught three to four months each year for nine years in this primitive pioneer cabin. Although her curriculum may have been elementary, the pioneer spirit of bettering oneself by learning to read no matter what social class one came from was taking root. Apart from the original colonies, which established schools with religious affiliations, settlers did not identify with this tradition. Therefore churches and schools were slow to take foundation in Kentucky. Nonetheless, early settlers believed firmly that to allow a man to reach maturity without being able to read, becoming functionally literate at best, was a sin in the face of God. Pioneers prided themselves on being able to spell and debate. Adults, as well as schoolchildren, frequently held spelling bees, which tested their ability to pronounce and spell words. It did not matter if the debater was knowledgeable about the topic, as long as a debater was imaginative and eloquent. Both spellers and debaters had their followings in the audiences, and the contests were as exciting as wrestling and shooting matches.

When the Coomes family moved to Nelson County in 1780, William garnered a first settler preemption of one thousand acres of virgin land. They settled in the outskirts of a village called Salem, which was later renamed Bardstown. The Coomes's choice of residence enticed a number of relatives and friends to relocate to Kentucky. The common belief that Maryland Catholics entered into a pact to settle together prior to 1785 is most likely true given their treks to the state becoming more regular after that date. Nelson County became a burgeoning enclave for Catholic emigrants after the arrival of a priest in 1787 and the establishment of a diocese in 1808. After the 1795 Treaty of Greenville ended much of the territorial disputes with Native Americans, Maryland Catholics flocked to pioneer settlements. By 1793 seven settlements in the surrounding Bardstown area boosted the local population to three hundred. By the time Bardstown was assigned its first bishop, Joseph Flaget, in 1811, more than one thousand families incorporated thirty congregations.

However, nativism, which favored the interests of established inhabitants over those of immigrants, was particularly directed toward anti-Catholic bigotry. With no central church of any denomination and little by way of Christian observances, frontier life threatened morality. Yet the solitary lifestyle of pioneers, the constant threat of Indian attack, and the underlying assumption that one was dealt whatever fate God rendered stimulated the reemergence of the Christian community by the time the Great Revival came to Kentucky. Although pioneer Catholics such as Jane Coomes remained unfazed by the ensuing religious revivals in nearby Cane Ridge, they settled in Kentucky without official papal approval to build a new spiritual enclave, eventually known as Nazareth.

Catherine Spalding

(1793–1858)

FOUNDER OF A CATHOLIC RELIGIOUS ORDER AND PROMINENT SOCIAL WORKER

Nursing cholera victims left Mother Catherine Spalding psychologically depleted. Mother Catherine and her community, the Sisters of Charity of Nazareth, had spent the last two-plus years tending to those sick and dying from cholera, putting their own health at risk in the process. Reverend Robert Abell advocated to Louisville city officials that the Sisters tend to cholera victims since there was a shortage of lay nurses to handle the epidemic. So nothing infuriated Mother Catherine more than hearing the accusation that the Sisters of Charity of Nazareth had been receiving city funds inappropriately. The accusation that the Sisters were mercenaries benefiting from the sick and dying was more than she would take.

She immediately fired off a scathing letter to Louisville's mayor, John Joyes, reiterating that the city council invited the "gratuitous services" of as many of the Sisters as necessary to relieve the public health crisis with only their expenses to be paid. However, the Sisters of Charity had been charged with profiting from nursing the sick. Mother Catherine proceeded to return the $75 stipend they received, closing her letter with a stinging remonstration that the Sisters "are not hirelings and if we are, in practice, the Servants of the poor, the sick and the orphans, we are voluntarily so, but look for our reward in another and a better world" (Doyle 2006, 105). Seventy-five dollars was a small fortune for the Sisters of Charity, who at the time had just completed a new orphanage and girls' school in Louisville. Joyes subsequently apologized, returned the money, and ordered a public correction. Not many women had the

Mother Catherine Spalding Sisters of Charity of Nazareth Archival Center

audacity to scold the presiding mayor of the state's largest city as Catherine Spalding had.

In 1795 Spalding's father, Edward, sold his inheritance of 112.5 acres in Charles County, Maryland, and moved to Nelson County when Catherine was two years of age. By the time she was five or six, Catherine's mother had died and her father subsequently remarried. Edward, burdened by the weight of supporting two families, mortgaged his land to settle gambling debts and eventually deserted the family. Edward's children and debts reverted to his sister and her husband, Thomas Elder. By the age of sixteen, Catherine had lived in four homes and resided in two states in the households of three fathers and four mothers, either biological or surrogate.

This disruption in her early childhood was balanced by the piety and humility of the Catholic community life. During the dead of winter in January 1813, Catherine was escorted by her cousin and cousin's husband on horseback to a log cabin at St. Thomas Farm to join two women, Teresa Carrico and Betsey Wells, in the formation of a new convent: Sisters of Charity of Nazareth. The congregation's origins were primitive and austere, living in a log cabin only eighteen square feet in area with one dining room and a half-story attic for sleeping. Meager furnishings included one frying pan, one spoon, and two knives. The simple residence was aptly named Nazareth. Being the middle of winter, the menu was limited to corn bread, middling (a dish made from coarse grain), and sage tea. Long days and demanding tasks, such as clearing land, took a mental toll on the three women, but evenings spent doing needlework fostered a bit of brief relaxation.

Aside from the daily work of spinning, weaving, and sewing for seminarians at St. Stephen's Farm, the Sisters made clothes for neighbors who would pay for them. Although poverty was prevalent on a daily basis, the community grew to six, prompting Father David, coadjutor bishop of Bardstown, to hold an election to choose their superior. Six months after its foundation, the six voted for their selection of nineteen-year-old Catherine as their first Mother to the Charity of Nazareth community, only the third religious congregation of women in the United States. Catherine dutifully served as general superior when called upon over the subsequent twenty-five years, and made most of the administrative and long-range-planning policy decisions affecting the Nazareth community.

Although the founding Catholic religious congregations in Kentucky were either emigrants from Maryland, native-born Kentuckians, or American converts to Catholicism, they were subjected to the prevailing attitude of nativism. Spurred by English propaganda, the nativism movement charged that Catholics could not be loyal American citizens because they were controlled by the pope. Roman Catholics were perceived to be enemies of the new republic out of fear that the pope would tighten his connections with European Catholic rulers who would attempt to cross the Atlantic and conquer the new republic. However, the leaders of the Roman Catholic Church in the young nation, such as Baltimore archbishop John Carroll, fervently believed in the American Revolution ideals of liberty and equality and passed these traits on to their religious protégés. American girls, whether rich or poor, should have the opportunity for an education, whereby upon completion of their formal education, they would extend their faith-based education to those less fortunate than themselves.

The Sisters of Charity of Nazareth's roots are founded on the principles of St. Vincent de Paul: humility, charity, and service to the sick and poor. The community took the virtues of American liberty and equality to heart, believing individuals should have equitability in all matters regardless of their political, social, or religious backgrounds. The community was fully supported by Kentucky bishop Joseph Flaget in this mission. Flaget personally brought over from France a rule St. Vincent de Paul had given to Elizabeth Ann Seton when she wanted to start an American religious community based on the French Daughters of Charity. Elizabeth Ann Seton founded the first American community of the Daughters (or Sisters) of Charity of St. Vincent de Paul. St. Vincent de Paul's rule advocated charity not only to alleviate suffering or deprivation but to promote human dignity in all dimensions. Along with a mission to serve those in need, the rule emphasized the need for letting the poor determine their own destiny and make an impact on their local community.

The Sisters offered an education beyond the traditional hornbook, dame school, or private academy curriculum of the era. Mother Catherine strongly supported a curriculum rich in science: botany, natural philosophy, optics, and chemistry. She argued to her superiors that parents, both Catholic and non-Catholic, would justify paying tuition for a rigorous curriculum, and those profits could then be supplanted in the education of orphans or other poor children. This stance did not always please the clerics, who were uncomfortable sending four or five female students over to the Nazareth men's college to partake in experiments at the physics laboratory.

Since Kentucky public schools did not have constitutional status until 1849, many private academies were administered by religious sects that were Protestant. As the state's population swelled, private academies couldn't handle educating the growing number of students, so many pioneers of Protestant persuasion sent their children to Catholic schools run by Sisters of Charity of Nazareth. Legal rights for nineteenth-century women were nonexistent; therefore, challenges existed for acquiring the land necessary for an addition to their first school at St. Thomas. In 1810 the Thomas Howard farm near Bardstown had been willed to two priests, Father Stephen Badin and Father Charles Nerinckx. The property was used to build a seminary, but by 1821 the Sisters were anxious to enlarge the building for their growing school.

However, the land on which the school resided was not part of the community. The Howard will deeded the land in two parcels. Flaget, trying to acquire all titles to church property, wanted both the Badin and Nerinckx parcels. Badin, fearful of passing debt-ridden property to the newly formed diocese, deeded to Flaget only one parcel: the one that did not include the bishop's house, the seminary, or the Sisters' home and school. The congregation could never own the land on which they built their school.

The crisis did not deter Mother Catherine because the following year St. Vincent's Academy in Union County was erected. With St. Vincent's Academy up and running, Catherine was asked to lead a mission in the diocese's "perennial seat of trouble," Scott County. Crises of land disputes, debt, and tempestuous relations between the French and English diocesan clergy seemed to follow Catherine wherever she went. For four months in 1823, Catherine and her company of three sisters and one slave cleared land, plowed, planted, and prepared for student enrollment at St. Catherine's Academy. Catherine faced opposition against the Catholic school by the predominantly Protestant residents and the pressure of mounting expenses brought on by educating students who were unable to afford the tuition and the inability to increase enrollment.

Up until this time, the Sisters of Charity of Nazareth had served the educational needs of the rural communities, but by 1831 Catherine was summoned to Louisville by Father Robert Abell to establish Catholic education for his parishioners. With a population of about ten thousand, Louisville was juxtaposed between racial and ethnic hostility amid Catholic indifference. It is amazing that within one year in a predominantly Protestant city, Presentation Academy attracted up to sixty students both Catholic and non-Catholic. This success was a blend of rigorous curriculum and Mother Catherine's skillful administrative policies with both parents and city officials.

Mother Catherine's zeal was pressed into service the following year when Louisville suffered from a severe flood, leaving many Louisvillians homeless or orphaned. Recalling her own early childhood when she was shifted between foster homes, Catherine took a personal interest in the plight of the orphans. She made trips down to the Ohio River levees to scoop up orphans left behind. She brought them back to Presentation convent, where the living conditions were crowded with six Sisters and children residing in a six-room building. Presentation closed as a school and the building was converted into an infirmary.

The Sisters, pressed for space as well as financial resources, decided to start a fair to raise money for food, clothing, and daily care of the orphans. Money raised by such fairs, chaired by former Nazareth students, was not the only means of support: It is well reported that Mother Catherine went on "begging" trips to squire money for the orphans. No matter how much money was raised, orphaned children kept coming to Mother Catherine, prompting the Nazareth Board to authorize Catherine to purchase property to house the St. Vincent Orphanage. Between

1834 and 1850 Mother Catherine supported 215 children, nearly all between the ages of one and ten, at St. Vincent Orphanage.

The number of cholera victims needing nursing care was substantial enough to warrant an infirmary off of the two wings of the orphanage. By the 1850s Catherine knew the time was right to separate the infirmary from the orphanage, so she steered her energy to negotiate property for sale on Fourth Street. Having built a network of city connections from both Catholic and non-Catholic laity, city councilmen, and wealthy businessmen, Mother Catherine solicited both financial resources and nursing personnel from both the Catholic and non-Catholic laity to establish the St. Joseph's Infirmary, which became the largest private hospital in the state. Established under the direction of Mother Catherine, St. Joseph's Infirmary completed the Vincentian fulfillment to care for the sick and the poor regardless of race, creed, or class until 1926.

From 1831 until her death, Catherine Spalding shifted her duties between St. Vincent Orphanage in Louisville and at Nazareth as general superior. In her last years Mother Catherine juggled priorities including a new establishment in Covington, renovation of the motherhouse at Nazareth, four new schools, and a new hospital amid a stressful break in the Sisters of Charity of Nazareth community in Nashville. The stress surely weakened Mother Catherine's health to the point that in February 1858, she contracted pneumonia while running an errand tending to a destitute family, and lingered for another few weeks until her death on March 20.

In November 2008 110 members of the Vincentian Sisters of Charity in Pittsburgh formally merged with the Sisters of Charity of Nazareth. The combined membership of more than seven hundred women will expand Catherine Spalding's mission of health care, education, and social services among five states, Canada, and India. Catherine's groundbreaking endeavors in health care, human services, and education are forever embodied by the academic curriculum taught to undergraduates at Spalding University.

Margaret Garner

(1834–1858)

SLAVE WHOSE TRIAL SPARKED CONSTITUTIONAL LAW DILEMMA ON STATES' RIGHTS

Sunday, January 27, 1856, was a frigid day in Boone County, where temperatures hovered between zero and twenty-six below. The temperature mattered little to seventeen slaves who were planning their exodus to Canada. Traveling full speed through the frigid night air, the group fled with a sleigh and two horses toward Cincinnati, stopping at dawn's first light. Fearing they would be spotted, the group parked their sleigh at Covington's Washington Hotel and started to cross the frozen Ohio River on foot. Upon reaching free soil, the group split in two: nine made their way uptown to a safe hiding place. The other eight slaves got lost asking for directions several times. Soon after the time the eight arrived at the home of Margaret Garner's uncle, freed slave Joe Kite, their trail was discovered by federal marshals.

The eight consisted of Simon and Mary Garner, their son Robert, Robert's pregnant wife Margaret, and their four children, all under the age of five. After feeding them breakfast, Joe Kite left to discuss with abolitionist Levi Coffin how to move the eight slaves through Underground Railroad stations. Simon, Mary, and Robert were the "property" of James Marshall of Boone County, whereas Margaret and her children were the "property" of Archibald Gaines, who resided down the road from James Marshall.

During the time Kite was absent, eleven sheriff's deputies identified his house. By the time Kite returned home at ten in the morning, the sheriff's deputies closed in and a crowd of twenty to thirty black and white residents watched as the standoff commenced. When the pursuers attempted to get Kite to open the door, he initially agreed, but then refused once he peered out the window and saw a swelling crowd surrounding his home. Five men began throwing chunks of firewood and smashing the windows. The remaining men forced entrance at the same time as Robert fired a round of bullets, resulting in the severing of one deputy's finger.

As the five deputies burst the door open, Simon fired three shots, striking one of the deputies in the finger and lip. Quick on the heels of their slaves' escape, James Marshall's son and Archibald Gaines made it to the house just in time to storm into the house and wrestle the pistol from Robert's hand. After Gaines subdued a bloodied but uninjured Robert, he and his posse proceeded to move into one of the rooms, stumbling upon a horrific scene. The body of three-year-old Mary Garner was lying in a pool of blood. Her throat had been slit to the point of decapitation. The two boys, Thomas and Samuel, were bleeding and crying—one had two gashes in his throat, the other a cut upon his head. However, the boys did not suffer the same fate as their sisters, having done their best to buffer their mother's blows. Nine-month-old Cilla was bleeding profusely from her nose and head, having been struck by a coal shovel. The pursuers entered a room precisely at the time Margaret, wielding a shovel, was to inflict a blow to the head of her infant daughter. Prior to the pursuers stumbling upon Margaret, she turned to her mother-in-law and frantically implored, "Mother, before my children should be taken to Kentucky, I will kill every one of them" (Weisenberger 1998, 74). Her mother-in-law said she should not do such a thing.

The resulting scene was chaotic and surreal. The posse had to hold back Robert and Margaret, who were attempting to attack each other. An inconsolable Archibald Gaines staggered out of the Kite home bearing little Mary Garner's body wrapped in a white shroud. Onlookers

"The Modern Medea—The Story of Margaret Garner" Library of Congress Prints and Photographs Division, Washington, DC

thought it odd that Gaines was so distraught over the child's death, concluding that he may have been the child's true biological father. If so, Margaret Garner inflicted a societal pain as severe as a physical one. She had struck the nerve cell of nineteenth-century misogyny by slaying her master's child. Gaines could not foresee this tragedy at the hands of one of his slaves, Margaret Garner.

Garner lived on Gaines's property, Maplewood, a sizable plantation owned by the well-connected Gaines family, whose members had served in Congress and in governorship of the Oregon territory. Born on June 4, 1834, Margaret Garner was born a slave of John P. Gaines, who had bought Maplewood when he was a politically ambitious lawyer and Mexican War hero. As a girl, Margaret Garner worked in that house, helping Priscilla care for the Gaines children. By age seven Margaret won trust and favor with her master and his family to the point that she joined the Gaines family on a two-day trip into free-soil Cincinnati. She certainly gained the amorous attention of the white men on the plantation, which was an unsettling but realistic problem for any female slave.

When John Gaines lost a reelection bid in 1849, he sold Maplewood to his younger brother, Archibald, and took an appointment as territorial governor of Oregon. Pregnant in 1850 with her first son, Thomas, Margaret married Robert in a move to ward off potential sexual pursuers. Since Robert's owner, James Marshall, hired Robert out to other plantation owners in neighboring counties, Margaret became more insecure over the erratic and belligerent behavior of Archibald Gaines. Suffering from bouts of depression, Gaines often took his frustration out on slaves, including Margaret, who bore a facial scar as a testament to his rage. With Gaines as the only white male on the plantation and Robert's long absences, Margaret's subsequent four pregnancies occurred during the time Gaines's second wife was not pregnant. In addition, three of her four children were light-skinned mulattos. Having experienced a brief sojourn on free soil, Margaret knew her future predicament was dire. If there was ever a time to escape, Margaret realized the time had come.

Surely Gaines could not envision that the infanticide by one of his slaves would spur a constitutional dilemma for the 1850 Fugitive Slave Law foreshadowing events leading to the Union divide. Under the Fugitive Slave Law, a slave owner had a legal right to seize his runaway slave without any court documentation. If this scenario occurred in a slaveholding state, there was never a problem. However, if the escaping slave was found in a free non-slaveholding state, it was not uncommon for a slave owner to come across abolitionists or authorities who would not cooperate with a slave's return to a slaveholding state. In these circumstances the slave owner obtained a certificate under the Fugitive Slave Law that barred interference with the transmission of the slave by any court or officer. If there was a fear that slave may be forcibly rescued from the slave owner, the master could obtain an affidavit and secure a

US district marshal to deliver the slave safely back to his or her master in the slave master's state.

The critical issue at the hearing under the Fugitive Slave Law centered upon whether the slave owed service or labor under the law of the state from which the slave escaped. Although legal action to obtain a certificate took place in a free state, no law of the free state could serve to emancipate the fugitive, thus the law of the slave state determined the outcome of the hearing. In many cases free and slave states disagreed as to the status of an individual claimed as a slave. Free states generally upheld that when a master took his slave into a free state, even without the intention to remain there permanently (as Gaines did with then seven-year-old Margaret), the slave could refuse to return. The master could not invoke the Fugitive Slave Law because the slave had not come into the free state as a fugitive. In circumstances where a slave returned voluntarily to the slave state, contention arose as to whether the individual had thereby reverted to his former slave status. The US Supreme Court held that in such a case the person's status depended upon the law of the slave state in which he found himself.

The Garners were brought to the federal courthouse in Cincinnati, where Gaines made application for a Fugitive Slave Law certificate to transport his slaves back to Kentucky. James Marshall's son neglected to get a power of attorney, so he could not act to reclaim his slaves. As a result the hearings were postponed. Since the slaves could not be sequestered in the courtroom, the district marshals took them to the city police station. No taxi would take the group for fear the crowds would destroy their cabs, so the group had to walk, a risky encounter among the tumultuous city streets. While the legal proceedings continued, friends of the Garners sought a writ of habeas corpus from Judge John Burgoyne's state probate court in order to try the detention of the slaves by US authorities.

The ensuing court case was not a simple trial. Up until this point Cincinnati courts upheld the ruling that slaves who were taken by their masters to live in the free state of Ohio were "emancipated" due to the fact that they resided under the jurisdiction of that state. Even if the slaves returned to a slave state, they remained "free," not lawfully recaptured as fugitive slaves. John Jolliffe, Margaret Garner's attorney, explained that in 1840 Margaret's former master, John Gaines, brought her to Ohio as a nurse for his infant daughter. Jolliffe's deposition highlighted the fact that her three surviving children were born in Ohio on free soil. Abolitionists and pro-slavery sides understood a habeas corpus battle was mounting: Federal courts had never before decided a case where human property committed a capital crime on free soil. Abolitionists questioned the legality of a property suit superseding a federal crime such as murder. Anti-abolitionists contended federal fugitive slave laws took precedence over state murder charges.

Jolliffe proposed that Margaret be tried for murder so that the trial would be held in a free state, offering her surviving children a chance to win freedom and Margaret to serve time in a penitentiary on free soil, rather than in the prison of human bondage. The trial dragged on for two weeks; a typical fugitive slave hearing would have convened within hours. By the start of the second week of trial, the courtroom audience swelled, as did the crowd of more than one thousand people outside the courthouse. Five hundred deputies were dispatched to maintain order on Cincinnati streets. The judge deliberated for another two weeks before delivering his verdict, siding with the prosecution that that the fugitives would have to be returned to their owners. He ruled that in order to win their liberty, the slaves had to assert their freedom while on free soil; however, they returned to Kentucky with their master, waiving their rights in the process.

Less than four weeks after their attempted escape, the Garners returned to Maplewood in early March. Prior to their release to their master, abolitionists attempted to strike a deal with Gaines to return the children to free soil. Gaines had paid a small fortune in legal fees and unfavorable press notoriety in order to win his "property" back, so the question remained as to how likely he'd be to give them up should Ohio Governor Salmon Chase persuade Kentucky Governor Charles Morehead to extradite the children, let alone Margaret. Nonetheless, Ohio authorities got an extradition warrant for Margaret to try her for murder, yet delays in delivering the paperwork to Morehead gave Gaines ample time to move Margaret between Lexington, Frankfort, and finally Louisville. By the time Ohio officials caught up with the Gaines entourage in Louisville, Margaret, Robert, and the children had already sailed two hours downriver aboard the steamboat *Henry Lewis,* bound for Gaines's brother's plantation in Arkansas.

Seventeen hours into their journey downriver, a passing steamer, the *Edward Howard,* plowed into the *Henry Lewis*'s starboard boiler, causing such an explosion that the *Lewis*'s bow was swept upstream. The aft section of the *Lewis,* where the Garners were shackled, began taking on water but surprisingly remained afloat. Set free, Margaret swaddled Cilla, moving toward the *Lewis*'s gunwale to attempt to board the *Howard,* which had nudged against the *Lewis*'s damaged bow to take on frantic passengers. Either by accident or seizing opportunity, Margaret and Cilla were thrown into the icy Ohio River. Two people jumped into the river to save Margaret, but Cilla could not be saved. It was reported that when Margaret was rescued, she displayed a joyful melancholy when told Cilla had drowned, the final reward for escaping the inevitable bondage to which Margaret would thus reutrn.

Cotton sowing had just started by the time the Garners reached Arkansas. However, two weeks after their arrival, Gaines's agent summoned Margaret back to Covington on the first available steamer. Pressured by negative press, Gaines was accused by northern newspapers of breaking his agreement to hold the adult Garners in northern Kentucky until Governor Chase's agents arrived with an extradition. A crafty Gaines had no intention of turning over a piece of human property he had paid so dearly for. So he moved Margaret from the Covington county jail to Maplewood, then to Frankfort, and finally to Louisville over the course of several days. For the second time in four weeks, Margaret had slipped away from Ohio agents, aboard *Eclipse,* shackled between barreled pork, kegged whiskey, and baled hemp. Attempting to regain his damaged reputation, Gaines published a letter in area newspapers noting he brought Margaret back to Kentucky as requested, but since Ohio "abolition avengers" never appeared to extradite her, and fearing "fanatics" might harm her, he was left with no option but to send her back to her family.

On April 17, 1856, Margaret disembarked from the *Eclipse* and rejoined her family. However, Archibald Gaines's brother feared that the Garner family notoriety might incite his own slaves, so he sold them to family friends in New Orleans. Less than two years later, Margaret met the same fate as her daughters. Her last words to Robert before slipping into a coma during the final stages of typhoid fever were "never to marry again in slavery, but to live in hope of freedom" (Weisenberger 1998, 278).

The Margaret Garner saga inspired a number of literary and dramatic art masterpieces including Frances Harper's 1859 poem "Slave Mother: A Tale of Ohio" and Toni Morrison's 1987 Pulitzer Prize–winning novel *Beloved.* The 2005 opera *Margaret Garner* premiered before sellout crowds in Detroit, Cincinnati, and Philadelphia. Touring Cincinnati's National Underground Freedom Center, one can find a painting by Kentucky painter Thomas Satterwhite Noble, *The Modern Medea* (see page 17), depicting the horror of slavery, which divided the nation more than 150 years ago.

Julia Marcum

(1844–1936)

ONLY RECOGNIZED FEMALE COMBATANT OF THE CIVIL WAR

In the twilight hours of September 7, 1861, as many as thirty-six Confederate rebels surrounded Hiram Marcum's house demanding he come out or they'd burn his house down. When their calls were unheeded, the rebels burst into Hiram Marcum's home using bayonets and threatening to kill the entire Marcum family. Hiram was not to be found inside since he'd been hiding on the fringes of his property on and off since the onset of the Civil War. When the Confederate army first arrived in Scott County, he felt it was safer to sleep outside than inside his home.

The sudden attack woke seventeen-year-old Julia, her mother, and four siblings from an unsettled sleep. The family was limited in what they could see because only one tallow candle burned, revealing that only one soldier remained in the house. Julia's sister Didama got hold of a match and lit the candle. Taunting the family with his bayonet, the soldier attempted to choke Mrs. Marcum. At that point Didama ran upstairs to get another candle. The soldier chased her upstairs, grabbed hold of her, and threatened to cut her throat and burn the house down. With that, Didama screamed for help. The only weapons in the house were two chopping axes; one claimed by Julia, the other by her sister Minerva. The hysteria inside the house prompted two men surveilling outside to race into the front door just as Julia went upstairs. At the same time Minerva threw her ax down, Julia lifted her ax up. Julia later recalled, "He struck me with the bayonet on his gun, I ran under

Julia Marcum on her ninety-first birthday Kentucky Historical Society

the gun, and chopped him in the face and breast with the ax, cut him to the hollow, and split his chin open with the ax, getting the best of him" (Kentucky Historical Society, 1926).

Knocking the gun right out from under him, the lone Confederate staggered around and cried out, "Don't chop me anymore." But Julia kept up her attack with wounded viciousness. Julia recounted, "I did not stop. He got hold of the gun and stuck the bayonet in my forehead, knocked my brains out, put out my left eye, and shot my third finger off my left hand" (Kentucky Historical Society, 1926).

Hiram was within earshot of the violence and could not stand by any longer. By the time Hiram made his way inside his house, he came up the stairs just as the gun fell out of the rebel's hands. Hiram delivered a fatal shot into the Confederate rebel's shoulder. Next to the dead rebel, his daughter Julia bled profusely and drifted in and out of consciousness. Amid the smoke-filled, blood-stained home, the assault ended. Julia recalled, "Father brought me downstairs, laid me on the bed, took his gun and went out of the house. All the rest of the rebels had run off" (Kentucky Historical Society, 1926).

The Marcum home sat within the tempestuous Scott County in Tennessee, which bordered Kentucky. Julia was born in Scott County on November 7, 1844. Hiram and his wife, Permelia, managed a farm on the Waters Buffalo Creek about four miles east of the Scott County capital seat of Huntsville. Julia inherited her resilient spirit from both her father's family, which descended from England, and her mother's side, the Huffs, descended from England and Ireland. Although anti-federal government sentiment may have been growing around them, Julia grew up in relative harmony among her four siblings, Clayburn, Didama, Minerva, and Martha. If his children were oblivious to the threat of secession, Hiram would not stand for such treason. Upholding the laws of the land was sacrosanct to an upstanding Christian man who proudly believed in the flag of American freedom.

The events that unfolded after the fall of Fort Sumter in April 1861 to the Confederates rocked the Tennessee-Kentucky border where the Marcums lived. While Scott County was formed in 1849 from other Tennessee counties—Anderson, Campbell, Fentress, and Morgan—many Kentuckians residing in McCreary, Wayne, and Whitley claim roots here. The Kentucky-Tennessee border was inaccurately marked by surveyors Dr. Thomas Walker and William Smith toward the north, and as a result the Tennessee River was positioned about seventeen miles north of the true latitude line. Kentucky accepted this erroneous Walker Line as an official border in early 1820, but significant parts of the boundary remained uncertain until a resurvey completed in 1859, some ten years after the formation of Scott County. Some settlers in the disputed strip were uncertain of which state they actually lived in.

Contentions between Kentucky-Tennessee border residents remained largely overlooked in Civil War history books. Civilian conflict, political manipulations, and slave resistance overshadowed any great battle or military leader. Neither Kentucky nor Tennessee supported Abraham Lincoln's presidential election. Secessionism reigned supreme in the western half of Tennessee but this sentiment was tinged with intimidation and coercion. Such volatility resulted in Tennessee becoming the last slave state to side with the Confederacy. Kentucky almost followed the same path but pledged allegiance to the Union in September 1861. Federal forces quickly understood the geographic, logistical, and political importance of keeping Kentucky Union.

Confederate rebels terrorized Union sympathizers in the counties straddling the sister states. Federal soldiers kept constant surveillance for both subversive women and guerilla rangers. Guerrilla rangers, such as legendary Confederate Champ Ferguson, intimidated and terrorized both federal soldiers and civilians. Scott County was strongly Unionist in sentiment but was eventually overcome by Confederates. It's no wonder that guerrilla warfare and random acts of terror left the Marcum family vulnerable to attack. Julia noted that, "When they [Confederates] mustered their armies and their people became enraged toward each other, [*sic*] tried to kill and destroy each other, and the Rebels invaded our county as there were but a few Rebels in the County. They sent their armies there to kill and destroy our men, women, and property" (Kentucky Historical Society, 1926).

The warfare conducted on this front pitted neighbor against neighbor along the Kentucky-Tennessee border. Many plainclothes mountaineers would partake in terrorist activities, living on the run and "laying out" in mountain gorges watching for opportunities to attack unsuspecting political targets or opponents. The Marcum family knew they were prime targets for Confederate rebels since Hiram was a "marked man" as an officer in the pro-Union Scott County Home Guards. Although the name sounds generic, home guards were little more than local vigilantes. In addition to his nebulous civilian activities, Hiram co-organized subversive missions to slip Union men into Kentucky who desired to join federal forces. The Marcum home was a place of embarkation. Confederate forces were determined to capture him, so a group of Confederate soldiers, dubbed "bull pups," stationed themselves a mile from the Marcum residence to keep tabs on any surfacing of Hiram. During their downtime they would drink, sometimes throughout the night. On learning that he was home, a squad of these soldiers surrounded the house to capture him.

None of this mattered by the time Hiram reached semiconscious Julia. She begged her father to hide for fear the marauders would return to kill him. In the meantime Julia's brother, Clayburn, sought medical assistance. Along the way he found the horse the dead rebel had ridden, so he got on it and rode to several houses begging for help. One woman, Mrs. Taylor, came to his aid. Clayburn turned the horse loose and the horse proceeded to go back to camp when daybreak came. Permelia sent Mrs. Taylor to tell the local Union captain of the attack, which prompted the captain to send a company of Union soldiers to the Marcum home. Realizing the severity of her wounds, the Union captain sent word back to his regiment to bring a doctor to the Marcum home. Although the medical assistance was necessary, Union soldiers entering the home to care for Julia put the Marcums in danger of being ambushed by Confederates.

Julia's rehabilitation took three months of being homebound. Traumatic injuries to the eye generally damage not only the eye but also adnexal tissues, visual pathways, and ocular tissues. Modern microsurgical techniques and prompt intervention can often restore some useful vision. However, such medical advances were not available to Julia. Around this time cocaine was sometimes used topically in eye surgery due to its antiseptic properties. However, it is more likely doctors treated any hemorrhaging with sutures to close the wound.

Within those months more danger followed. Hiram made an attempt to move back into the home, but Confederate rebels stalked and ransacked the property. In one incident Julia and her cousin, Union soldier George Marcum, were shot by rebels. A sniper's bullet creased Julia's scalp but deflected and killed George. At age fourteen Clayburn was neither old enough to join the war nor strong enough to withstand another possible break-in. By January 1862 the burning of their home forced Hiram to move his family to Williamsburg, in Casey County, Kentucky, nestled in the Appalachian Mountains. Hiram joined the 13th East Tennessee Union cavalry and started his march to the sea. However, he got as far as Nashville and succumbed to smallpox. Hiram's personal property was destroyed during the war, and his land was sold for taxes after the war. The title to the property was removed from the family for failure to redeem it from sale.

Julia and her family lived on the Green River for a while, then moved to Flat Lick in Pulaski County, Kentucky. Permelia passed away shortly after the end of the war. Julia finished her education and supported herself as a teacher for twelve years. However, the wounds she suffered that fateful September night ultimately plagued her to the point that she could not teach. Her siblings moved on with their lives: Didama eventually married a doctor, and Martha and Clayburn married local Casey County residents. Whether or not Minerva's marriage to the brother of Union Colonel Frank Wolford had anything do with it, Julia petitioned Congress in 1884 to receive a disability pension. Wolford, by that time a decorated veteran, was a member of the House of Representatives and supported Julia before his fellow legislators. He noted, "I saw Julia A. Marcum shortly after she was wounded, and have known her well ever since her wound. For a few years after the war she supported herself by teaching school; but disability from her wound has continually increased until her mind is seriously impaired and her health so completely destroyed that she cannot support herself. She has no means and is as helpless as a child" (Reports of Committees: 48th Congress, Second session, 1885).

A number of witnesses and neighbors of Julia corroborated Wolford's testimony. On October 15, 1885, Congress approved a special act granting her a pension of $30 per month in recognition of her meritorious service. The committee remarked, ". . . this daughter of a brave soldier, who gave his life to his country, who, when just entering womanhood, received an injury in defense of her person and that of members of her family from outrage at the hands of a Confederate soldier which renders her an invalid for life, should receive a pension, and therefore recommend the passage of the accompanying bill" (Reports of Committees: 48th Congress, Second session, 1885). In September 1922 her pension increased to $40 per month, making her the only female combatant recognized during the Civil War.

Julia lived long enough to see soldiers leaving and returning from Europe during World War I. She outlived her siblings and most Civil War veterans her age. During her lifetime she was the only female who was a full member of the Grand Army of the Republic of America, of which she was a member for most of her ninety-one years. The Grand Army of the Republic of America (GAR) was an influential organization of Union veterans of the Civil War. Having inherited her father's law-abiding spirit, Julia's membership was particularly poignant given the GAR's fervent views on secession as treason, slavery as a curse, and the nobility of war sacrifices for the country's liberty. When she died on May 5, 1935, Julia was buried with full military honors at Highland Cemetery in Williamsburg, Kentucky. She was the only female Civil War veteran.

E. Belle Mitchell

(1848–1942)

FOUNDER OF THE KENTUCKY COLORED ORPHAN INDUSTRIAL HOME; FIRST AFRICAN-AMERICAN TEACHER AT CAMP NELSON

The night of her first day of class, African-American teacher Belle Mitchell was escorted to the Camp Nelson dining hall with Brother Fee, who offered her a place to sit. Once she sat down, the table occupants were aghast. Most of the American Missionary Association workers, Freedmen's Aid Society workers, and assorted female camp teachers refused to sit near her. A regional chaplain from Maine and several army officers admonished Fee for bringing Belle into the dining hall, to which Fee replied, "I will suffer my right arm torn from my body before I will remove this young woman" (Sears 1996, 30). This reply hardly softened the hall steward, who then retorted that his wife would not serve Belle a plate. Undeterred, Fee replied to the steward, "Then she will have mine, and I will have another" (Sears 1996, 30). Fee figured his action would spark a more Christian spirit to the table occupants.

However, Fee's assessment of the situation was naive. Commanded by a Methodist minister and the camp commander, Colonel James Jacques, to remove Belle from the dining hall, Fee held his ground. Jacques recommended Fee take Belle down to the soldiers' quarters until the situation settled down. Believing the time had come to break down racial prejudice, Fee asserted, "I will risk all with the issue" (Sears 1996, 30). Jacques summoned Fee, accusing him of setting off a maelstrom within the staff over the inclusion of a Negro in the common area, and going so far as stating Fee would eventually face retribution by the

AMA. Unfazed, Fee asserted he would not back down in his position to support Belle's integration into the staff common areas. Infuriated that a civilian would fail to heed the request of the camp commander, Colonel Jacques retorted, "I will have nothing to do with it. I will leave you with the mess" (Sears 1996, 30).

Fee and his small group of supporters attended meals every day, but his opponents waited until Fee's group left before they would go into the dining hall. The climax after several weeks of this defiance arose when one of the anti-Fee contingents addressed a letter to Fee admonishing him for not letting the missionary staff know about Belle's hiring and forcing him to require her to dine at the soldier's dining hall.

This incident was hardly unusual to E. Belle Mitchell, the daughter of former slaves who bought their own freedom. Raised in a strong religious household, Belle's parents sacrificed what little money they had to send her to private schools in Xenia, Ohio, and Danville, Kentucky. In the fall of 1865, abolitionist John Fee, serving as a missionary for the American Missionary Association, visited Belle's Methodist church in Danville, Kentucky. He was so impressed by Belle's reputation in the ministry that he contacted her parents so he could hire her as the first African-American teacher at Camp Nelson. He explained to her parents that her service might produce "un-Christ-like" opposition, but her gifts and talents would rise above such opposition. Belle's parents consented and with that Fee escorted eighteen-year-old Belle to a Camp Nelson dormitory. She started teaching the next day.

Camp Nelson was a Union army supply depot critical to the military operations focused in eastern Tennessee. Toward the war's end, Southern emancipated slaves seeking refuge up north came to Camp Nelson to join the Union army. This surge of ex-slave recruitment resulted in Camp Nelson becoming the largest recruitment facility for the United States Colored Troops (USCT). Camp Nelson not only became the training center for freed slaves entering the Union forces but also an epicenter for

The Colored Orphans Industrial Home, July 10, 1931, from the Collection on Lafayette Studios The University of Kentucky Photographic Archives

African-American soldiers' families who had been expelled from their former masters' property once they had been manumitted. Army commanders were overwhelmed by more than 2,400 African-American women and children living as squatters around the camp's perimeters.

Union personnel turned the camp over to AMA workers whose task it was to educate and provide medical assistance to the refugees. Founded by blacks and whites alike, several freedmen's relief organizations began to form across the country, resulting in the emancipation of slaves. Friction among organizers of these groups prompted them to split up into many other organizations. When Reverend John Walden of the western branch of the American Freedmen's Aid Commission (AFAC) rankled with the eastern branch, he withdrew from the organization entirely. Walden took with him several Methodist members to form the Freedmen's Aid Society. With this split, he secured a vast number of schools and associated teachers belonging to the western and northwestern branches of the AFAC. What was left of the eastern branches of the AFAC folded into the influence of the American Missionary Association's western branches.

The American Missionary Association was founded by New York City businessmen and abolitionists Arthur and Lewis Tappan and sought an end to slavery sooner than the laws of the country could be passed or battles could be fought. The AMA sent agents to follow Union armies that were advancing through Confederate territory and set up schools to bring both Christianity and literacy to freed slaves. By 1867 more than thirty-eight thousand students and 525 teachers were enrolled and employed in AMA's schools—a true testament to the organization's vision. Two years later the organization founded eleven colleges for former slaves.

Fee attempted to integrate the camp teaching staff, with the inclusion of Belle Mitchell as his test case. If Fee had any preconceptions about the racial tolerance of his peers, those were now dispelled, for it was clear that the majority of his "Christian" missionaries were guilty of race phobia. One of Fee's more vocal opponents, Reverend Lester Williams Jr., wrote a letter to Fee stating tersely, "Your introduction into this house and to the table of a woman of color, without the consent of the occupants of it, and of those who conduct the mess, excites much comment and repugnance to the act" (Sears 1996, 30). However, Fee did have supporters, one of whom, Reverend Scofield, observed that the very people "who could not bear to eat in the same room as Belle Mitchell had no objections to employing half a dozen black faces to wait on them at the table and brush off the flies" (Sears 1996, 31). Such rancor would have dismayed any eighteen-year-old, but Belle continued to work in the hostile environment, providing a challenging life lesson Belle would need to fall back on later in life.

At a crucial point during this maelstrom, Fee left the camp to tend to family matters in Berea. During that time, on September 14, 1865, Colonel Jacques removed Belle Mitchell and other Fee supporters from Camp Nelson. Further insult occurred when Jacques demoted Fee as superintendent of the camp refugee home but gave the position to the wife of Reverend Williams. Fee later learned that Williams was filling in as acting superintendent during his absence. This final act of intolerance disgusted Fee so intensely that he eventually left Camp Nelson and focused his efforts on the founding of Berea College, the accomplishment for which Fee is best known. Fee did apply to the AMA for Belle's rightful teaching pay and appealed to the organization to set some standard for how the organization would handle the sensitive racial issue for its employees. After several weeks the AMA sent agents from Cincinnati down to Camp Nelson to assess the situation. The contingency decided all AMA teachers would sign a disclosure declaring that "they would not make complexion a condition of association among teachers"(Sears 1996, 33). The measure did not fare well with all AMA employees, as Fee noted, "those who did not sign were wormed out after a long time of working" (Sears 1996, 33).

Although Belle was forced to return home after three weeks at Camp Nelson, her premature dismissal was foretelling because by October 20, the refugee school closed permanently when the War Department closed Camp Nelson. By early November Fee placed Belle in charge of a Freedman Bureau's school for children of black soldiers in Lexington and recommended her for an AMA commission. She opened the Lexington school with twenty-eight students and enrolled another sixty-nine students four months later. Her roles in increasing enrollment and winning the praise of her superiors were constantly juxtaposed with an environment of white hostility toward educating former slaves, inadequate classrooms, and a lack of school supplies.

Nonetheless, life pressed forward for Belle. She took a break from teaching and went back to school in 1867 at Berea College, the first interracial coeducational college in the South. In 1871 her marriage to Jordan Jackson proved to be a dynamic coupling. Jordan Jackson was a former slave who became a successful Fayette County businessman who owned undertaking and livery businesses. Self-taught and a fervent advocate for education, Jackson presented a bill to the 1886 Kentucky General Assembly to create a normal school to train African-American teachers, currently known as Kentucky State University. Belle supported and worked alongside Jordan in all his business and political efforts. Although she co-operated a millinery business in Lexington, her most significant contribution to the African-American community occurred when she founded the Colored Orphans Industrial Home in 1892.

During an eight-year period after the Civil War, cholera was spreading throughout major cities in the United States. As the epidemic spread, the number of orphaned children began to rise. African-American families were particularly hard-pressed. A small contingent of female African-American civic leaders, including Belle Mitchell, took notice of the abundance of homeless black children roaming Lexington's streets and founded the Colored Orphans Industrial Home.

When it first opened its doors in 1894, the COIH admitted four women. Rules for admittance were strict. Recommendation for admission was required by a physician, an admission committee member, or six references that could vouch for the applicant's character. With the average admission age of seventy-two years, no person could be admitted into COIH if there was an immediate relative or friend who could provide similar care. In an effort to maintain its reputation in the community, COIH would not accept anyone who would not adhere to the COIH ground rules. In its early years, COIH provided food, shelter, and clothing to indigent elderly women ranging in age from sixty-four to eighty-five years, but the age of residents eventually reverted to those of homeless children.

COIH managers were proactive not only to educate their residents but also to provide them with a skilled trade in order to become self-supporting. The mission of COIH eventually shifted toward preparing younger residents to become self-sufficient adults. Adoption was also an arm of COIH, but it was not the first option for children.

COIH managers would regularly subcontract younger residents to private homes or businesses so that they could learn or work in a trade. In fact, Belle Mitchell often took one child at a time to apprentice at her Lexington millinery. Eventually, the COIH began to offer a lucrative tailoring and shoemaking department that provided residents with some of the state's first vocational training.

COIH encouraged the "learn by doing" curriculum practiced by peer schools Tuskegee Institute and Hampton Institute. A November 1900 feature in the *Lexington Morning Herald* highlighted the COIH modus operandi: "Each week three to four girls are taken in charge by the head of the culinary department and outside of school hours are taught all that can be put into their heads about the art of cooking, so that finally every girl-child in the institution has a fair notion of this important matter. Even to the very little ones are assigned such domestic tasks as they can fulfill." Educating and providing vocational training for orphaned children to become skilled workers was unheard of at that time and even higher minded in comparison to today's foster care.

By 1909 COIH served residents in two buildings on eighteen acres. Between 1915 and 1950 the tailoring and shoemaking training slowly died, leading way to the 1980 name change to the Robert H. Williams Cultural Center. Williams, a Fayette County businessman, bequeathed fifty-five acres to the COIH at the time of his death, and the organization shifted its mission from destitution to community service responsible for the educational, social, and recreational needs of all children in Fayette County.

Belle Mitchell died on October 6, 1942 in Lexington, where she is interred at Greenwood Cemetery. One woman's refusal to be dismayed by racial intolerance parlayed into the formation of a social service agency and a forerunner to the twentieth-century civil rights movement.

Captain Mary Garretson Miller

(1846–1894)

FIRST WOMAN TO EARN A RIVERBOAT PILOT'S LICENSE

Erie No. 10 owner Blanks Line submitted a formal complaint to the board of Steamboat Inspection Service in New Orleans that the *Saline* was out of compliance with the law since Captain George Miller was acting as both master and pilot. The board contacted Captain Miller about the complaint, which prompted him to have his wife, Mary, apply for her pilot's license. Hoping to thwart competition, Blanks Line erupted over the possibility of the *Saline* being piloted by a woman. Never mind that Mary Miller had navigated the *Saline* along the Red River countless times alongside her husband. The Steamboat Inspection Service board in New Orleans stalled on making a decision about whether or not a woman could obtain her pilot's license, eventually passing the decision making on to SIS headquarters in Washington, D.C. The agency had never encountered this situation before.

Mary Millicent Garretson was indoctrinated into life on the river by her steamboat engineer father, Andrew, and his wife, Luanna, since her birth in Louisville's Portland neighborhood. Upon marrying widower George Miller on August 3, 1865, Mary was a quick understudy, helping George build and pilot steamboats such as *Saline.* Building a business and raising four children, Lula Ann, Georgia, Emma, and Norman, was not customary for a nineteenth-century woman. George was a river pioneer himself, having been the first to build a flatboat and take coal down the Mississippi from below Owensboro to the La

Mary Millicent Garretson Miller: line illustration based on photograph by Washburn, which appeared in Harper's Illustrated Weekly, *March 8, 1884* Portland Museum, Louisville, KY

Branche sugar plantation, just about thirty miles north of New Orleans, in 1829. Dubbed "Old Natural Miller" for his river expertise and artisan craftsmanship, George developed a respectable business building smaller draughts that carried passengers and freight on the smaller rivers, such as the Red, Black, and Ouachita Rivers, which large tonnage steamboats were too cumbersome to navigate. Basing his operations out of Louisville was critical for George given Louisville was one of three major centers for steamboat construction in the West. The other two centers were Cincinnati and Pittsburgh. Steamboats built in any of these three ports were identified by their distinctive vertical high-pressure engines.

Between 1820 and 1880 nearly six thousand steam vessels, weighing in at over one million tons, were built between the Mississippi and Ohio River corridor. In one year the average weight of one hundred boats was eighteen thousand tons. Pittsburgh, Cincinnati, and Louisville steamboat operations accounted for nearly three-fourths of that number and more than four-fifths of the tonnage of steamboats traveling US waterways during the 1880s. Steamboat builders in this region needed to consider the difficult waterway conditions, which impacted travel efficiency and safety. Master craftsmen such as George Miller were well aware of the role floating logs, sandbars, direct landings at riverbanks, weatherization of wood by sun and ice, and the tremendous weight of engines exerting high pressure played on steamboat performance and durability. A skilled pilot understood the Mississippi and Ohio Rivers ran swift and fluctuated in depth. A steamboat with two thousand tons of freight needed to draw six feet of water to cruise safely. In the early years of steamboat building, designers with only deep-sea shipbuilding experience built boats with double frames. After the 1840s such design became impractical in low water and riverbank debarkation, so steamboat builders added a flat bottom with a single frame, reducing the weight of the vessel.

Unlike shipbuilding in the East, steamboat builders in this region did not use oak timber due to its poor durability and rapid decaying properties, opting instead for straight-cut timber. Although straight-cut timber was cheaper, it was also weaker due to the cross grain in crooked pieces cut from straight-grained wood. Steamboat operators more often than not exceeded recommended weight limitations, disregarded high and low water levels for hull members, and wore out engines and machinery. As much as these factors impacted the steamboat industry, they supplied a steady pace of employment for craftsmen such as George Miller. Louisville made a name for itself in the industry by being a port for cabin building, steamboat machinery, and boiler construction.

The design of western steamboats may not have contributed to their speed or durability as much as their eastern counterparts, but they were prized for their passenger comfort and decor. Ranging as large as forty-five feet in diameter, wheels were built aft to each engine side to balance the engines forward and give proper engineering alignment. Constructing a long, strong hull (as great as 130 feet) would move a ship twenty-five miles an hour downstream or eighteen to twenty miles an hour upstream. Hulls of such length were critical to hauling the immense quantity of coal that was mined from the upper tributaries along the Ohio River down south. The typical engine revolution was fourteen or fifteen revolutions per minute, cited by one *Popular Mechanics* reporter at the time as "all that was necessary to send a big steamboat forward at a swifter speed than any contemporary deep-water-ship"(Eskew 1929, 442). High-pressure engines may have produced a slower speed in the water, but they were built to outlast the ship itself. The disadvantage of high-pressure engines was the high rate of ship explosions. In a seven-year time period, 213 steamboat accidents claimed the lives of 2,304 and injured 956 people.

Nearly thirty-five years younger than her husband, Mary often assisted George with piloting the 178-ton *Saline* through altering river channels, shifting sand bars, and caving banks and snags. She also served as the business's bookkeeper. Running a steamboat business was a family affair, and George's son from his first marriage served as an engineer. The work the Millers put into their business eventually paid off. By the 1880s the steamboat industry reached its peak. George Miller's reputation had made its way as far south as New Orleans, and his competitors did not want him to enter the steamboat market there. In March of 1883, when George and Mary were running their customary route between New Orleans and Bayou Mason, George was reported to the Steamboat Inspection Service (SIS) by an anonymous person who charged that he had been serving as both the *Saline*'s master and pilot, a serious breach in steamboat law. With the steamboat industry being highly competitive, breaches in regulations could be financially devastating for the Millers. When the SIS confronted George, he confirmed that he had in fact acted as pilot, but his wife, Mary, acted as the master. George told the regulatory agency that Mary would be applying for her license and be fully tested.

There wasn't much choice for Mary but to take the exam. When Mary first approached the Inspector of Hulls office in New Orleans, she was told, "But, Madam, how can we 'captain' a lady?" (Curry 1983, 201) Mary knew her expertise understanding the importance of slack and shoal water, staying close first to one bank and then the other, according to the pattern of flow of the river. She mastered the river language of reading every point, stump, limb, ridge, rock, or snag. Navigating landmarks above and below the river determined a skilled versus a novice pilot. Along with the written examination, Mary needed to prove to the New Orleans SIS steamboat inspector her ability to handle emergencies and potentially threatening circumstances.

After eight months with no decision rendered, New Orleans inspector George L. Norton didn't know what to do. He felt it socially improper for a woman to take a position usually given to a man, believing the situation would in turn be degrading to a woman. To avoid making a decision, Norton passed her application on to the secretary of the treasury at SIS headquarters in Washington, D.C., whose initial reply to the application was, "Has Mrs. Miller a husband living?" (Kleber 2001, 621) By December the Treasury Department's inaction on a decision prompted several national newspapers, including the *New York Times,* to track the situation, often penning newspaper articles with heavy sarcasm against the agency.

The media attention may have been one factor that helped Mary Miller win her pilot's license. Secretary of the Treasury Charles Folger telegraphed the New Orleans SIS board "that Mrs. Miller be granted a license if fit to perform the duties required, without regard to her sex" (Kleber 2001, 621). Mary passed her examination and was formally granted her master's license on February 16, 1884, at the age of thirty-eight. Folger's telegram duly noted that he "objected to the issue of the license upon social grounds, as having a tendency to degrade the female accepting such license" (Curry 1983, 288). This social snub hardly dimmed Mary's limelight once the news media found out. Her picture appeared in the March 8, 1884, issue of *Harper's Weekly.* In May 1884 Elizabeth Cady Stanton wrote about the controversy, "If we press Mrs. Miller and her steamboat . . . into the compass of syllogism, and prove logically that 'United States citizens' have a right to choose their own wives and employments, half the writing and speaking in this country as to class privileges might be ended" (Gordon 2006, 355).

Though fame was fleeting, Mary operated steamboats over the subsequent four years along the Mississippi River Valley. As master of the *Saline,* Mary was responsible for all daily operations and financial reporting. The Millers maintained two homes: one onboard *Saline* in New Orleans and another in the Portland neighborhood of Louisville. Under George's tutelage, Mary proved to be a skilled steamboat captain. Her own experience growing up in the field sharpened her skills as a shrewd but effective businesswoman, as noted in New Orleans's newspaper river columns in the 1880s and 1890s.

However, George's advancing age and the decline of the steamboat business prompted the Millers to return to Louisville. In 1891 George had tired from the steamboat industry, and his timing coincided with the rise of the railroad industry. The growing national economy at the onset of the industrial age prompted the shipment of both goods and services quickly and efficiently. Railroads had an impressive advantage of speed over steamboats. Railroads could cover greater mileage at a faster speed than steamboats.

This difference was no more obvious than comparing the time spent shipping freight and passengers between the two. In the late 1850s a steamboat loaded with freight and passengers departing from Louisville for St. Louis took two days and twelve hours. Even if the railcar was loaded with only freight, the same trip from Louisville to St. Louis via railroad took fourteen hours. A railcar loaded with passengers from Louisville to St. Louis took one day. In addition to speed, rail transportation operated with greater punctuality than steamboats. Steamboat travel was still seen as comfort travel at the onset of railroads, which initially were known as dirty, noisy, cramped, and poorly ventilated. However, the time saved in rail transportation more than compensated for increased transportation charges and creature comforts for businesses.

George and Mary decided to make their permanent home back in Louisville at the Bank Street home George had built for Mary as a wedding present. When they returned to Louisville, they began building a new sailboat, the *Swan,* to sail in their retirement years in the Gulf of Mexico. In 1891 the Millers sailed south down the Mississippi River for a winter sojourn, making it as far as the jetties at its mouth. However, they needed to have the *Swan* towed back to Louisville by the coal boat *W. W. O'Neill.* It was not George who fell ill, but Mary. When Mary died three years later, George kept his residence on the *Swan;* he couldn't bear to return to the Bank Street home he had shared with Mary.

Although Mary had obtained her pilot's license to keep her family business afloat, in the process she advanced the role of women in maritime trades. She was posthumously honored as the first American woman to receive a steamboat master's license in the American Merchant Marine Hall of Fame in 1993 and two years later in the National Rivers Hall of Fame. Only a handful of women have received similar honors.

Enid Yandell

(1870–1934)

GOLD MEDAL RECIPIENT FOR WORLD'S COLUMBIAN EXPOSITION

Bertha Palmer, Chicago art patron and former Louisvillian, introduced Enid Yandell to her niece Julia Grant, widow of President Ulysses S. Grant, during a reception after the unveiling of the Grant Fountain in Chicago.

"Let me present to you Miss Wendell, the young sculptor; she is at work on the Women's Building and we are very proud of her and think we have conferred on her an honor," Palmer said, turning to Grant.

"I don't approve of women sculptors as a rule," Grant remarked. "I don't disapprove of you, Miss Wendell," she added gently, "but I think every woman is better off at home taking care of husband and children. The battle with the world hardens a woman and makes her unwomanly."

"And if I had no husband?" Yandell replied.

Grant stated, "Get one."

"But if every woman were to choose a husband the men would not go round; there are more women than men in the world," Yandell said.

The former first lady retorted, "Then let them care for brothers and fathers. Will your stone cutting make you a better housewife?"

"Yes," replied Yandell. "I am making muscles. Then I can beat biscuits when I keep house." (Loughborough, Hayes, Yandell 1892, 104-105)

This exchange was hardly unusual for Enid Yandell, a single woman living in the late nineteenth century. What was unusual was the fact that Enid Yandell was a classically trained sculptor who was a rising star in the art field, soon to bask in the limelight as one of three women to receive

Enid Yandell with a group of small sculptures The Filson Historical Society, Louisville, KY

the 1891 gold Designer's Medal for her female caryatids upholding the roof garden of the Women's Building at the Chicago World Columbian Exposition. Enid was one of a rarefied group of six female sculptors to debut their works for the Chicago exposition. At age twenty-two her remarkable entrance into the predominantly male field was bold and brazen given that many male sculptors vied for the chance to showcase at this national venue, yet a woman took away the top award.

However, Enid Yandell was more or less born into the field. The daughter of a Louisville physician and artist mother, Enid was exposed to the interplay of art and anatomy at an early age. She graduated from Louisville's Hampton College, majoring in chemistry and art. Greek gods and goddesses captivated Enid, and she proceeded to take a first-place medal for her senior prize, a statute of a Greek god, upon graduating in 1889 from the Cincinnati Academy of Art. After graduation she toured Europe with her mother and sisters, studying statuaries of prominent citizens in its town squares. In the summer of 1891, armed with a number of referrals from family friends, she submitted her application as the official sculptor of the Women's Building at the Chicago World Exposition. Bertha Palmer, president of the Board of Lady Managers at the exposition, was thrilled to hire a woman and recommended she start immediately. Under the apprenticeship of sculptors Lorado Taft and Philip Martiny, Enid and several other male and female sculptors worked from five in the morning until six in the evening designing sculptural decorations to accent the fairgrounds. Aside from the long work hours, Enid handled up to two thousand pounds of clay for her meager wage of five dollars per day. However, Enid's persistence and talent paid off when she was awarded a gold Designer's Medal as well as influential contacts.

National attention from her success in Chicago encouraged her to move to New York, where she established a studio serving as an assistant to Karl Bittner. During her stint she designed adornments for the

Astor and Vanderbilt homes and an intricate facade of Philadelphia's Pennsylvania Railroad station. Yandell won her first public commission from Louisville's Filson Club by designing a seven-foot statue of Daniel Boone, which graced the Kentucky state building at both Chicago's World Exposition and the Tennessee Centennial Exposition before taking permanent residence in 1906 standing guard at Louisville's Cherokee Park. She used Boone's actual hunting shirt, flintlock rifle, tomahawk, scalping knife, and powder horn in the design. As Yandell's rendition of Daniel Boone resides in the midsection of Kentucky, a copy of Yandell's statue depicting Boone guards the eastern part of the state on the Eastern Kentucky University campus.

In the winter of 1894, Yandell left the United States for further study in Paris. She began studying with both Auguste Rodin and Frederick MacMonnies, an expatriate American sculptor schooled in Beaux-Arts style, exhibiting regularly in Paris salons. Emulating larger-than-life characters of the classical antiquities, Enid began work on a twenty-five-foot plaster copy of the Louvre's *Athena* to serve in front of the reproduction of the Parthenon at the 1897 Tennessee Centennial and International Exposition in Nashville. Although *Athena* gracefully watched over the exposition for six months, she was not bronzed and was ultimately destroyed due to weather. As much as public attention focused on the colossal Pallas Athena, Yandell won a silver medal for her *Allah-il-Allah* figurine, which modeled a Hindu at prayer.

Upon returning to her New York studio, Yandell was inducted as the first female member elected into the National Sculptor and Municipal Art Society. Her induction into the prestigious National Sculpture Society afforded her highly visible commissions such as the *Carrie Brown Memorial Fountain.* All her training in Paris was poured into the bronze and granite memorial given to the city of Providence, Rhode Island, by Italian Paul Bagnotti in memory of his wife in 1899. Twenty feet tall and thirty feet at the base, the fountain was celebrated for the then novel idea of water coming up at the base instead of down the center. Although the fountain was an experiment in size and scale, Yandell noted each figure represented certain life struggles from which one tries to free oneself (e.g., duty, passion, soul). Such spirituality drew mixed reviews: It received an honorable mention at the Pan-American Exhibition in Buffalo, but was dubbed in one review as "confusing, but certain features of the struggling group are very fine indeed" (Taft 1903, 451).

Publicity for the *Carrie Brown Memorial Fountain* garnered Yandell numerous city contracts commemorating iconic heroes, heroines, or mythology starting with Louisville's *Hogan's Fountain,* which featured mythical Pan playing his flute for four terrapins. Her sculptures featured prominently on the cover of *Harper's Weekly Magazine, Harper's Bazaar,* and *Ladies' Home Journal,* in addition to scores of national newspapers. She also collaborated with George Grey Barnard to prepare a sculpture for a New York theater. Over the course of her career, she had exhibited in twenty-seven major shows, with her most endearing works permanently residing in public parks. Smaller pieces including busts and reliefs are housed in public and private repositories from Rhode Island to Missouri. Her last public commissioned piece was the kneeling statue of Chief Ninigret, the sentinel of the harbor in Watch Hill, Rhode Island.

Caught in Paris during the onset of World War I, Yandell's career took a radical shift. Unable to return to the United States, Yandell, along with four other female artists, organized the Appui Aux Artists committee to solicit funds to operate a canteen to feed impoverished French artists and their families. They used the Pavillon de Flore section of the Louvre to store food and supplies including an American shipment of canned pork and beans. The rules were fairly simple—applicants were interviewed and given a ticket representing a week's worth of meals—and the canteen managed to serve up to one thousand impoverished French artists and their families per day. To keep the canteen afloat financially, the committee tapped wealthy Americans such as railroad magnate E. H. Harriman, financier Otto Kahn, and Edward Harkness, who cabled not only money but often also clothing. Yandell also dually served with the Red Cross and La Société des Orphelins de la Guerre, which cared for French war orphans.

Upon her eventual return to the United States in 1915, Yandell continued her social work by establishing an index of hospitalized soldiers while serving as the director of the Communications Bureau of the American Red Cross. She conducted a rigorous speaking tour, visiting women's groups in Cincinnati, New York, Boston, Louisville, and Chicago and drumming up financial support for French orphans. But by the 1920s, Yandell all but disappeared from the public eye. Yandell actively supported the women's suffrage movement and even campaigned for Calvin Coolidge, but made few public comments about her art other than to comment that sculpture was "a lovely occupation for a woman." However, she maintained her interest in art by establishing a summer art school, Branstock School of Art, on Martha's Vineyard, which operated until her death in 1934.

Her humbleness in the profession masks the prominence of her reputation in the world of art. In June 2006 one of her six-foot-tall sculptures mysteriously disappeared from the grounds of a historic Tenafly, New Jersey, apartment building. Local artist Alice Renner Rigney brought the sculpture's significance to the Historic Preservation Commission's attention. Rigney became interested in the piece when she began putting together an art show depicting the town of yesteryear. As she conducted research for the art show, she found a letter written by a former Tenafly native who reflected on the sculpture signed by Yandell. "I felt when I first heard about this last spring that, gosh, that's something the town should know about," she said. "These are nice things that give you a pride of place" (Sangha 2006).

Patty Smith Hill

(1868–1946)

KINDERGARTEN REFORMER; "GOOD MORNING TO ALL" SONGWRITER

In 1933 Irving Berlin and Moss Hart opened their Broadway production *As Thousands Cheer.* The revue, featuring a compilation of music, dance, and satire, drew its vignettes from the lives and affairs of the rich and famous of the day. Behind the satiric barbs that mimicked Queen Mary, John D. Rockefeller Jr., and Josephine Baker, a childlike ballad titled "Happy Birthday" was sung and became an instant hit. However, when Jessica Hill heard the song, she immediately recognized the melody. "Happy Birthday to You" was not a song available for anyone's use. The melody was a carbon copy of "Good Morning to All," a song published by Jessica's sisters, Patty and Mildred Hill, in 1893. She was tired of her sisters not getting compensated for their melody that songwriters, producers, and Hollywood stars were performing.

The Broadway production was hit with a bombshell: a copyright lawsuit filed by Jessica and her sister Patty. "Happy Birthday" sounded distinctly similar to the kindergarten ballad Patty and her older sister, Mildred, had written titled "Good Morning to All." The Hill sisters successfully proved to the court that there were undeniable similarities between "Good Morning to All" and "Happy Birthday," making them the official copyright holders. The family became the legal owner of the song and beneficiaries of the royalties whenever the song was performed. Although Mildred's music career was cut short when she passed away in 1916, Patty Hill experienced the apex of her career as a professor of education at Columbia University.

Patty S. Hill University of Louisville Photographic Archives

When Patty and Mildred Hill were both teachers at Louisville's Experimental Kindergarten, they wrote "Good Morning to All" as a simple greeting for teachers to welcome students into the classroom. Patty wrote the lyrics; Mildred, an accomplished pianist and organist, wrote the music to the tune. The song was published in a book titled *Song Stories for the Kindergarten.* The lyrics to "Good Morning to All" eventually were published in Robert Coleman's 1924 songbook, but a second verse was added. During the mid-1930s the tune was tweaked some more but appeared in the Broadway musical *The Band Wagon* (1931) and as the promotional piece for Western Union's first "singing telegram." All the while the sisters never received compensation for its use.

Simple melodies similar to "Good Morning to All" were frequently sung to Patty Hill and her six siblings by their mother. Martha Hill was an avid poetry lover and would incorporate songs to encourage her six children to complete their daily chores. Patty's father, Dr. William Hill, was a Presbyterian minister and editor of the antebellum *Presbyterian Herald* before switching careers. He established the Bellewood Female Seminary in Anchorage before taking a position as president of Fulton, Missouri's Female College. Born in 1868, Patty was raised to appreciate nature and explore many subjects thought unsuitable for women at the time, including geology, math, logic, astronomy, and philosophy. Patty and her siblings were encouraged by her parents to pursue careers that would give them economic independence. Such direction ran counter to the practice of the day.

Advocating advanced education, Patty graduated from Louisville's Collegiate Institute in 1887 and enrolled in the only kindergarten-training class in the city. Another Louisvillian, Anna Bryan, had spent time in Chicago training and operating a free kindergarten program. Anna came back to Louisville to start a new training school and free kindergarten association in the city. Bryan was excited to be part of an alternative kindergarten program that was not based on the traditional methods of Friedrich Froebel. Patty Hill was one of Bryan's first graduates and was hired onto the staff of the Louisville Training School for Kindergarten and Primary Teachers. Bryan let Patty take over a kindergarten class and thus more experimentation began with incorporation of additional activities and play into kindergarten instruction.

During the 1860s and 1870s, kindergarten was first introduced in the United States and educators followed the teaching methods of Friedrich Froebel. Froebel, a German educator, believed that children learn best through self-activity or free play. Envisioned as a tool for both educational and social reform, the Froebelian theory emphasized that a teacher should not drill children in lesson content, but encourage self-expression through individual or group play activities within pleasant natural surroundings. His educational philosophy relied on manual training to unite mind and body and a thorough study of nature with a heavy slant on Germanic ethnicity.

Although Anna Bryan drew some of her teaching methods from Froebel, she disliked the rigid sequence of rote kindergarten games such as small blocks, thin sticks, sewing, and pasting activities. She believed such games were artificial and lacked spontaneity. Her kindergarten reform movement, championed under G. Stanley Hall, challenged the Froebelian approach to kindergarten instruction, which attempted to mold the child into the adult world. American kindergarten educators from the 1890s to World War I started to abandon some of the Froebel's teaching methods, which concentrated on self-activity and physical training amid controlled natural surroundings, at the time American cities were experiencing an influx of immigrants who were living in congested urban dwellings. Although Froebel's pedagogy emphasized universality, urban kindergarten teachers had difficulty Americanizing immigrant students who were not ready to set aside their multiculturalism. American kindergarten education, especially during the rise of immigration, was designed to thwart crime while fashioning proper citizenship, not necessarily preparing children for excelling in grade-learning outcomes. In fact, kindergarten education during this time had been mocked for being equated with beautiful classrooms, spacious school grounds, and pedagogically trained teachers.

Anna Bryan and Patty Hill attended one of developmental psychologist G. Stanley Hall's child study movement summer classes at Clark University between the summer of 1894 and 1896. As a new approach to applied psychology, child study took an evidence-based approach to analyzing children's fears, habits, predilections, and cognitive skills in the classroom. Hall began to see that Froebel's emphasis on the manipulation of small motor objects, such as sewing, might actually cause fatigue and medical problems in children. After a series of seminars held around the country, Hall's child study research started to gain interest in prominent educators of the era including Bryan, Hill, Alice Putnam, Kate Douglas Wiggin, Nora Archibald Smith, and Lucy Wheelock.

Hill and Bryan believed the Froebelian approach was sterile for child learning. The women believed allowing children free play and a naturalistic approach to learning eventually equated to productive adult work and positive ingenuity. Given Hill's own Presbyterian upbringing, she parlayed the role of child play as both democratic and a gift from God. Both women believed that teacher lectures did not influence child learning. Free play allowed the teacher to see the whole child: strengths, weaknesses, needs, etc. However, Froebel's method of instruction, which was originally created for German students in rural settings, did not make sense for Louisville's urban kindergartners who came from the poor sections of the city. The natural setting for most of these immigrant children was anything but controlled natural surroundings; they lived in overcrowded, polluted, and even squalid conditions.

This approach was apparent during one particular classroom circle time in which Hill attempted to teach a particular topic. One of her students interrupted and asked, "Teacher, who are you talking to anyhow?"

(Jammer 1960, 68) After that incident Hill began to incorporate the urban and street vernacular students attending the Louisville Training school were used to hearing. Particularly impressed by the theories of Colonel Francis W. Parker and John Dewey, Patty began to study up on the leading educational child psychologists and their work. In fact, Parker, the head of Chicago's Cook County Normal School and early education reformer, made a trip to Louisville in 1891 and was impressed by the curriculum at the Louisville Training School.

Anna Bryan returned to Chicago in 1894 and became a principal of the kindergarten normal department at the Armour Institute. Upon her departure Bryan appointed Patty principal at the Louisville Training School. Patty quickly established herself as one of the leaders in the progressive movement in American education. During her seven-year tenure, Hill expanded kindergarten classes from one class to eight. She increased enrollment in LTS's initial teacher-training classes from five to fifty. By 1905 Hill's innovative work in Louisville gained the attention of Columbia University's Teachers College dean, James Russell, who invited Hill to lecture there on her kindergarten research. Hill was not the sole speaker invited to lecture that year—she shared a podium with Mary Runyan and Susan Blow, both Froebelian followers. Hill was invited back to Columbia the following year and eventually was asked by Russell to join the college's faculty permanently. This appointment meant Hill would challenge the Froebelian kindergarten approach taught by most of the Columbia faculty members.

Patty Hill led kindergarten reform over the next three decades. To test her liberal theories in contrast to existing conservative Froebelian methods, Russell allowed Hill to establish an experimental Speyer school "play" room at the Teachers College for children ages three to seven with no previous school experience. Hill created a social laboratory to survey children as they solved problems or played creatively, generating a movement that would abandon Froebelian materials and replace them with materials based on activities relevant to the child's experience. She became department chair in 1910 and developed the curriculum at the university's Horace Mann Kindergarten. The program highlighted three phases of development during the kindergarten year: vocabulary increase, combining words to make a clear statement, and reciting songs, verses, or stories from memory. She wrote, "I don't believe there's a normal school in this country without one of our graduates substituting the new ideas for the old" (Rudnitski 1995).

Although she rarely wrote scholarly literature, Patty Hill was responsible for the publication of research she personally believed in. She was the editor of *Experimental Studies in Kindergarten Education* and *A Conduct Curriculum for the Kindergarten and First Grade*. Her leadership in evidence-based scholarly research led to her part in the founding of the university's Teachers College in 1924, the Institute of Child Welfare Research, and the National Association for Nursery Education. By the time public schools adopted kindergarten programs nationwide, Hill began a new initiative introducing nursery school education at the Teachers College in 1922. Stemming from her strong developmental psychology approach, Hill believed kindergarten and nursery schools could provide the foundation for psycho-social health and well-being.

Hill saw the need to unify kindergarten and primary instruction but was opposed to the idea of using kindergarten as the means to indoctrinate prereading. When John Dewey became head of Columbia University's Department of Philosophy, Hill incorporated many of his socialization and moral theories into her education pedagogy. She was also awarded full professorship and was appointed head of the college's department of Kindergarten Education in 1922. Hill intertwined free child play and socialization into classroom instruction, even introducing the "Patty Hill blocks," which were so large children could design structures tall enough to fit inside. Aside from "Happy Birthday to You," the Patty Hill blocks are one of her claims to fame to this very day.

Infusing theories of developmental psychology and behavioralism in education, Hill recorded the Teachers College laboratory children's individual and social progress reports during a six-year period to gauge desirable habits and traits in children. Hill then sought up to four hundred early childhood education specialists to devise a list of specific habits that children should form as well as the activities and subjects needed to develop these habits. Co-written with psychologist Agnes Rogers, Hill published a book of eighty-four kindergarten habits in 1923 titled *Tentative Inventory of Habits,* which was implemented at both the Teachers College as well as various schools around the country including the University of Chicago. This list became the basis for modern kindergarten curricula and afforded Hill an honorary Litt.D. degree in 1929.

Among Hill's greatest contributions in the field of education was the Manhattanville Project. This joint venture (with the Teachers College, Union Theological Seminary, Jewish Theological Seminary, and Juilliard School of Music) attempted to revive New York City's Manhattanville section beginning with the establishment of a nursery school called Hilltop Community Center, which operated between 1932 and 1938. During the middle years of Hilltop's establishment, Hill was awarded the first female professor emeritus from Columbia University in 1935. She died in 1946 following a lengthy illness. Although her contributions to the field of education were meritorious, Patty Hill's claim to fame is a simple morning kindergarten song. Warner Communications, now known as Warner/Chappell, purchased the copyright in 1989 for more than $28 million. "Happy Birthday to You" is the most performed song of the twentieth century; its copyright is not set to expire until 2030.

Sophonisba Breckinridge

(1866–1948)

FIRST WOMAN TO PASS THE KENTUCKY BAR; NOTED SOCIOLOGIST; FIRST WOMAN TO EARN A J.D. AT UNIVERSITY OF CHICAGO

Sophonisba Breckinridge noted on her report for 4500 Paulina Street, "Cellar floor covered with sewage water. Man claims four feet in some places. Needs attention at once. Plumbing in whole house bad" (Fitzpatrick 1994, 180). On another visit to a tenement home, Breckinridge noticed one of the children had "diseased eyes," prompting her to contact the United Charities of Chicago to ask them for a referral to the Illinois Charitable Eye and Ear Infirmary for the child. These were just a few of the many reports Sophonisba Breckinridge compiled as a non-salaried Chicago tenement inspector in the Chicago Department of Health. In 1908 Breckinridge, along with her colleague Edith Abbott at the School of Civics and Philanthropy, was tapped by Chicago's chief sanitary inspector, Charles Ball, to assist in surveying city housing. This was exactly the type of work both women readily engaged in so that their graduate students could witness how social research could impact social reform.

Such bleak circumstances contradict the distinguished early years of Sophonisba Breckinridge. Born in Lexington, Kentucky, on April 1, 1866, she was the second daughter of Colonel William Breckinridge, a former Confederate officer and lawyer, and Issa Desha, a member of a well-respected Kentucky family. Her parents had the means to educate all their daughters but also expected them to be dutiful to family and unselfish in virtue. Breckinridge started to make a name for herself when she became the first woman to matriculate at the high school

Sophonisba Breckinridge (1866–1948) The University of Kentucky Photographic Archives

preparatory academy at the University of Kentucky in 1882. Dismissed from Agricultural and Mechanical College of Kentucky (now the University of Kentucky) admission for being a woman, Sophonisba's parents understood she would benefit from a rigorous education, so they contacted family friend and Wellesley College founder Henry Fowle Durant, persuading him to admit her. Her tenure at Wellesley College came at the same time as many educational barriers for women were beginning to wane. Two years later she enrolled at Wellesley College, graduating with a degree in mathematics.

Once Sophonisba achieved her Wellesley College degree in 1888, she taught high school in Washington, DC, during her father's tenure in the US Congress. Confused over what she wanted to do with her life, William Breckinridge confided to her, "You ought to look squarely in the face that if I die, you will have to make your own living; and if I live you may have to do so anyhow"(Fitzpatrick 1994, 6). Keen on pursuing a career in law like her father, Sophonisba returned to Kentucky to help with family responsibilities and read law in her father's law office after her mother's unexpected death. By fall 1892 she felt confident she could pass the Kentucky bar exam, so she traveled with her brother Desha into Frankfort on business. The chief justice of the court of appeals (a former colleague of her father during the Civil War) and two colleagues grilled her for more than four hours, eventually agreeing she was qualified to practice law. They administered the oath required of members of the Kentucky bar to Sophonisba. By the following Monday, she was formally introduced to the Court of Lexington: Kentucky's first woman ever admitted to the bar.

Her accomplishment made the front page of the *New York Times,* but all the accolades did not render a slew of legal work. During the downturn of her legal practice, Sophonisba visited a Wellesley classmate at the University of Chicago who introduced her to the dean of women, Marion Talbot. Talbot offered Breckinridge a job as her assistant and encouraged her to complete a fellowship to study political science and economics. The University of Chicago attracted many female applicants due to its availability of financial support for graduate study and its appointment of older female proprietors to oversee younger female students. Breckinridge attained her Ph.D. in political science and economics magna cum laude in 1901 and was ready to market herself in academia.

However, tenured track professorships did not come as easily for Sophonisba as they did for her male counterparts. Academic positions for female economists were rare due to the fact that economic departments were hesitant to hire women, who were stereotyped in the nineteenth century as passive, soft, and domestic in contrast to the field of economics, which was viewed as a hard, logical science. While her male counterparts succeeded securing university research positions, Breckinridge was stuck living in a dormitory as an assistant while she obtained her J.D. through the University of Chicago's 1904 first law school graduating class, making her the first woman to earn her J.D. degree at UC.

Breckinridge's luck changed when Marion Talbot sought her as an assistant professor in University of Chicago's newly created Department of Household Administration. Sophonisba taught a Legal and Economic Position of Women course, which intrigued one of her students, Edith Abbott. Edith and Sophonisba began a professional partnership that lasted more than ten years. Between 1905 and 1915 Breckinridge wrote six scholarly journal articles focusing on women, employment, and labor law. Two of these articles, focused on the legal aspects of female industrial employment, caught the eye of leaders of Chicago's reform movement including Jane Addams. Addams was well aware of the interplay between citizenship, democracy, and women's relationship with the two through work at the Hull House. Hull House reformers transfixed their efforts on labor reform and protection for low-wage workers, many of whom were immigrants. Breckinridge considered it a privilege to be tapped by female reformers to conduct research on their reform movement while earning valuable publishing experience to break into academia.

The timing of these publications corresponded with the emergence of the twentieth-century Progressive Era reforms. These reforms were rooted in the belief that women who were raised as citizen workers will in turn raise productive citizens as long as the government proactively supports citizenry through protective legislation in child care, labor laws, wage equity, and sanitation and health standards. This belief was an outtake of Breckinridge's experience working in Jane Addams's Hull House and her burgeoning role in Chicago's reform community. She joined the Chicago Women's Trade Union League devoted to helping working-class women organize and improve workplace conditions. Over the next fourteen years, she spent part of her vacation each year living at Jane Addams's Hull House. This volunteerism was met with consternation by her family since her father forbade her from becoming a settlement worker.

In addition to teaching at the University of Chicago, Breckinridge began teaching at the Chicago School of Civics and Philanthropy and became dean in 1909. She enticed Abbott to join its administration, transforming its program from a typical vocational social work curriculum (customary for its time) into an empirical professional degree similar to law and medicine. Breckinridge and Abbott intended to influence the next generation of social workers as proponents of industrial labor reform. The pair required students to pursue courses in statistics and social research methods in order that these skills could be used to persuade social legislation. Both women were eager to make a name for the new school as a research mecca, so they garnered research contracts from various agencies (e.g., Russell Sage Foundation, the federal Department of Labor, and local health authorities) to entice an elite group of students. In 1911 and 1912 the department supported thirteen students by such contracts, and throughout 1910 students were publishing articles from their research.

Breckinridge steered her students toward finding alternative financial assistance for low-income women, a possible outtake of Breckinridge's own graduate dissertation on the legitimate right of the federal government in regulating economic affairs. The women conducted two nationally recognized studies, the first being a door-to-door survey of Chicago's tenement housing whose findings were published between 1910 and 1915 in the *American Journal of Sociology*. The second major study collected and investigated thousands of Chicago's juvenile court cases and interviews between 1899 and1909. The culmination of this empirical research resulted in the title *The Delinquent Child and the Home.* The research concluded that poverty and civic neglect, not the role of the individual and family, were the roots of most urban problems. Breckinridge demonstrated to her students the role of using their professional training to encourage legislative social reform.

Even at this time it was generally well known that employment would be scarce in the field without a degree. The School of Civics encouraged full- and part-time students, many of whom worked in social service agencies. During the 1914–1915 term, 180 out of the 193 registrants were women who took part-time classes. Some college coursework or the equivalent of a GED was all that was required for admission. For those who could not afford the full tuition of $75, more than eleven scholarships and ten "research studentships" were offered. Curriculum was split into three key departments: general training, social investigation, and social museum, library, and publicity. A typical practicum for a student entailed an assignment to work fifteen or more hours per week at a Chicago social agency in addition to ten to twelve hours of classroom instruction. Supplementing field work were tours of inspection at stockyards, tuberculosis sanitariums, recreation centers, settlement houses, and Cook County Hospital. Students were required to complete two-thirds of their coursework in investigation and the remaining one-third in social research and methodology.

No doubt her tenure as a tenement and factory inspector led Breckinridge to believe that African Americans suffered the brunt of urban problems. Breckinridge believed African Americans had more difficulty escaping the blight than many immigrants did, so she joined a variety of organizations committed to racial advancement, including being an early member of the Chicago branch of the National Association for the Advancement of Colored People (NAACP), the Association of Colored Women, and the Chicago Urban League. Breckinridge was instrumental in securing funds from Sears Roebuck magnate Julius Rosenwald to build the Wendell Phillips Settlement and two scholarships to the School of Civics and Philanthropy for black women.

Two factors prompted Breckinridge to join forces with the University of Chicago. First, she lacked an endowment to proceed building the Chicago School of Civics financially. Second, the academic merit aligning her program with an esteemed institution such as the University of Chicago could not be passed up. In 1915 Breckinridge suggested that the school's board of trustees seek affiliation with three local Chicago universities: Northwestern, University of Illinois, and the University of Chicago. Although the University of Chicago expressed interest, negotiations broke down when World War I began and negotiators went off to war. However, by 1920 the university explored a plan for a graduate program in social work and negotiations resumed.

In August 1920 the Board for the School of Civics signed a contract to bring the School of Civics and Philanthropy formally under the University of Chicago's auspices, thus creating the Graduate School of Social Administration, the first school associated with a major university and furnishing a PhD degree. Breckinridge and Abbott were both appointed associate professors in its new School of Social Service Administration. The partnership did not benefit all of the School of Civics students. After the transfer the University of Chicago refused to accept the School of Civics programs for recreation specialists or public health nurses. In addition, the university's program was a graduate program, which meant many associate or undergraduate School of Civics students would not be able to pursue the curriculum at this level. Many School of Civics students were part-time students employed in agencies, with minimal if any undergraduate degrees and little if any money to take graduate courses. Breckinridge felt opportunities still existed for these students, stating, "in general persons for whom for some time to come there will be considerable demand by agencies whose funds are limited and whose work has not been raised to a high-level of professional efficiency" (Muncy 1994, 80).

By this point, Breckinridge rested on the success that she was shifting social work toward reform and professionalism, winning respect within Chicago reform-movement leaders. Her civic involvement included a role as co-founder of the Chicago's Immigrants Protective League and vice president of the National American Women's Suffrage Association. Breckinridge's reputation as a scholar, author, educator, and reformer afforded her positions within the Consumer's League, the American Association of University Women, and the Women's Peace Party. When she participated in 1911 and 1915 strikes by Chicago garment workers, she furthered the efforts for compulsory education laws, the minimum wage, the abolition of child labor, the establishment of the Federal Children's Bureau, and the state's right to remove children from abusive parents.

Although she never earned status as an economist or lawyer, Sophonisba Breckinridge used her educational training toward social and civic reform, which was not a commonly held belief in early-twentieth-century academia. The turn in her professional career came after her creation of the Graduate School of Social Administration when she was named department chair and awarded full professorship by 1925. This solidified her reverence in the storied halls of the University of Chicago until her retirement in 1942. She spent her retirement years working on her autobiography. On July 30, 1948, Sophonisba Breckinridge passed away after suffering from a perforated ulcer and arteriosclerosis.

Nannie Helen Burroughs

(1879–1961)

SOCIAL ACTIVIST; ESTABLISHED PRIVATE SCHOOL FOR BLACK WOMEN; FOUNDER OF LOUISVILLE WOMEN'S INDUSTRIAL CLUB

A few years had passed since Nannie Helen Burroughs opened the doors in a rented building to members of the Women's Industrial Club, charging little more than ten cents for admittance. Club members served lunches to African-American workers in downtown Louisville, then finished the day taking millinery, sanitation, children's hygiene, sewing, and various other classes in domestic science subjects. Whatever money for club events wasn't brought in from student tuition, Nannie earned or covered out of her own pocket.

One day one of Louisville's society matrons came into Women's Industrial Club inquiring if Nannie was running a cooking school. When Nannie confirmed she was, the woman asked how she was paying for it. Nannie replied, "We club women pay ten cents a week, make pies and cakes and sell them." The society matron replied, "Well, don't give your lessons for nothing any longer. People value more highly that which they pay for. If they can afford only a penny, let them pay that. I will pay you for every pupil you have, so that you can get whatever you need for the school" (Hammond 1922, 51). This benevolent gesture was all Nannie needed to spark interest in the club. Eventually, increased membership prompted Burroughs to hire additional teachers and workers. Once removed from the classroom, Burroughs set her eye on a loftier goal: a school that taught black girls economic self-sufficiency, religious piety, and self-esteem. Little did Burroughs realize that her idea for a same-sex

Nannie Helen Burroughs, 1909 The Rotograph Company

school would actually become a prototype for black entrepreneurship and women's rights.

Born in Orange, Virginia, in 1879, Nannie Burroughs was the daughter of ex-slaves. Her father was a carpenter and itinerant preacher who passed away in her early years. Her mother, Jennie, desired a better life for Nannie than the impoverished conditions many African Americans were living in. So Jennie took five-year-old Nannie and moved to Washington, D.C., to live with her aunt Cordelia and attended the best school Washington had to offer an African-American child. Nannie attended M Street High School, a well-respected African-American school, where she graduated with honors in 1896. She took her high school years seriously by taking business and domestic science courses, believing she could find an assistant teaching position upon graduation. Although her private life was marred by the loss of her father and sister, such setbacks failed to sidetrack Nannie's ambitions.

The teaching position she worked so hard to win was not to materialize. She later found out the position was given to someone who had connections with the employer. "I can't tell you how it broke me up," Nannie acknowledged. "I had my life all planned out—to settle down in Washington with my mother, do that easy, pleasant work, draw a good salary, and be comfortable the rest of my life, with no responsibilities to weigh me down" (Hammond 1922, 48). Another more likely reason for the hiring choice, which Nannie never publicly acknowledged, was that her skin color was too dark for the position. Washington's African-American community ranked its own social prominence on a color line. Light complexions were favorable for public positions, a fact that was supported by the number of Washington African-American schools whose teachers and administrators were light-skinned. Denied a chance for a position she felt she deserved, she decided that one day she would open her own school in Washington that would welcome girls of all abilities. But that dream would have to wait a while.

Finding work as a typist and stenographer, Burroughs moved to Philadelphia, and after a year she moved to Louisville to take a position as bookkeeper at the headquarters of the National Baptist Convention of the Colored Church and also edited the *Christian Banner.* At the time, black Baptist leaders believed African Americans needed to take charge of their own Christian influence and advance not only their race but the kingdom of God. A devout Baptist and astute businesswoman, Burroughs took charge of both the male and female sides of the church's business affairs. Whether teaching Sunday school classes or hosting the biennial meeting of the National Association for Colored Women, Nannie felt a strong twinge that something still was missing. She once said, "If you're going to be a Christian, you've got to do something week-days as well as talk and feel about it Sundays" (Hammond 1922, 50). With that, she organized the social and charitable Women's Industrial Club in 1900.

Years of classroom instruction perfected one of Burroughs's gifts: exceptional oratory skills. During the annual meeting of the Colored Baptist Convention, she spoke with such fervency that she was elected secretary of the Women's Auxiliary, the missionary arm of the convention. During her first year as secretary, the auxiliary raised $1,000. By 1920 Nannie succeeded in raising more than $50,000. When she felt her influence in the organization was sustained, Nannie decided the time was right to broach the subject of a girls' school with auxiliary membership.

Burroughs's concept of a same-sex academy was not new. Tuskegee Institute, Hampton Institute, and the Institute for Colored Youth were other examples of same-sex schools. However, these comparable academies were generally funded by whites. Burroughs felt confident that African Americans could financially sustain a same-sex school by themselves. However, she could not support it herself, so she proposed the venture to the Women's Auxiliary. Much to her chagrin, the auxiliary felt such a school should be geared toward missionary efforts for the Baptist Church as a whole. The group prided themselves on a three-year capital campaign that raised $13,000 for a building in Africa. The women favored an idea to rent space for bringing African girls to the United States and train them for missionary work. "That's not my idea," said Nannie. "It must be national, not Baptist—something all colored women can do for all colored girls"(Hammond 1922, 53).

Undeterred, Nannie persuaded the auxiliary to form a site-search committee. With the auxiliary's blessing, Burroughs traveled to Washington during the summer of 1907 to search for a location for the school. Advocating the school be located in the nation's capital, Burroughs settled on a dilapidated eight-room house with a bucolic view that rested on a hill in northeast Washington. Six acres surrounded the home, offering plenty of room for growth, but at a price of $6,500, Nannie needed to go back to Louisville to negotiate the finances. Before she left Washington, she paid the $500 deposit with her own money. Upon returning to Louisville, many tried to convince her to build a school there, but Burroughs maintained her conviction and returned to Washington with the full $6,500 in 1909.

The National Training School for Girls and Women opened in October 1909 with eight students. Burroughs was its principal, chief financial officer, and development officer throughout its first fifty-two years. When the school attempted to increase teachers' salaries, Nannie solicited donors. With the school situated far from its initial funding source, the Women's Auxiliary slowly withdrew support for the school, leaving Burroughs in financial straits. When it appeared closing its doors might be imminent, a Richmond, Virginia, banker named Maggie Walker came to Burroughs's rescue. She gave $500 to the school with the express condition that she remain anonymous. This gift did not go unacknowledged—Burroughs dedicated a building in Walker's honor.

Beyond its first few tumultuous years, NTSGW flourished. The outlying buildings that dotted the campus's ample acreage were eventually turned into dormitories and classrooms. Concrete was laid for walkways and new basements. Additional classrooms were constructed during World War I. Although financial backing came from whites, the local black community supported the school's mission. A northern Baptist white woman donated $3,500 for a domestic science classroom; blacks donated $500 to outfit the classroom. Beneficiaries came from all over the country. In fact, Burroughs received a surprise phone call from a banker in California telling her she was bequeathed $1,000 from the estate of a wealthy white gentleman who gifted funds for any African American who showed vision and initiative. The local African-American community donated $3,000 to build and house a four-thousand-volume library for community and student use.

Success did not come without hardship though. During World War I the water pump went out during the dead of winter, prompting staff and students to retrieve water from local springs. In addition to water, staff and students carried coal up to the main entrance when the coal company suffered from a shortage of deliverymen. Everyone tended pigs and chickens, laundered their own linens, and prepared their own meals. "I think the hard years were the best ones we had," Burroughs reminisced. "We built more character. Souls grow under character" (Hammond 1922, 59).

Burroughs emphasized NTSGW was not a reform school for wayward girls. It was no secret that NTSGW would not enroll girls who were delinquent at other schools. Such behavior was not only intolerable, it was believed by Burroughs that it served no purpose in elevating the African-American racial profile. Since its inception, Burroughs advocated welcoming colored students of all backgrounds starting at age fifteen, but most applicants came from working-class African-American families. Cited as nondenominational, the NTSGW initial application specifically asked whether or not applicants were Christian. If applicants were not interested in a religious education, it was best not to apply.

Letters of reference and recommendation for both applicant and applicant's parents were required along with the $5 NTSGW application fee and a certificate from a dentist vouching for the applicant's oral condition. Every new student underwent another dental and eye examination after enrollment. Entrance exams in English and math were required. NTSGW students maintained an 80 percent proficiency among their courses or faced the possibility of being removed. Students who earned a 75 percent or higher cumulative average were moved to the next grade. By 1933 Burroughs added a "children's department" equivalent to junior high school for girls ages eight through twelve that emphasized the cleanliness of both mind and heart.

A firm believer in self-help, Burroughs offered no tuition scholarships. However, a few students completed work study positions within various campus departments to help pay for their tuition. These positions were restricted to students age seventeen or older who were healthy and reliable. All books and supplies had to be purchased on the first day of school; anyone without a textbook on the first class was not officially enrolled. NTSGW attracted students from all over the United States and abroad, especially Africa and the Caribbean. The school equally hired Christian teachers who were upstanding members of their community, which offered parents assurance that their daughters would be aptly cared for during their enrollment at NTSGW. By 1929 NTSGW had enrolled more than one hundred students.

With an emphasis on domestic science, Burroughs was well aware of the primary occupations her graduates would take. Nicknamed "the school of three B's—Bible, bathtub, and broom," the moniker reiterated Burroughs's standards for spirituality, cleanliness, and service. NTSGW offered courses in Bible study, tailoring, millinery, music, printing, cosmetology, practical nursing, and missionary work. Such courses were typical for the jobs relegated to most blacks at that time: hairdresser, manicurist, dressmaker, midwife, laundress, and housekeeper. Conversely, the curriculum maintained rigorous courses in advanced math, foreign language, history, and even Negro history. Intellectual superiority was not a goal at the NTSGW, but economic viability and service to others was emphasized in its liberal and industrial arts education. NTSGW prepared students for careers, whether low income or not, which provided students a means of economic sustenance. Burroughs fervently believed that even if employed in domestic service, NTSGW students should serve their employers well in the same manner as they themselves would want to be served.

The school enlightened Burroughs to realize African-American women needed to come together to work toward improving their standard of living, improving their self-efficacy, and serving God. This was evidenced by the fact that the school was mostly supported by the African-American community. In the initial eleven years, $232,000 cash was raised for the NTSGW, which was renamed the National Trade and Professional School for Women and Girls in 1934. Of that amount, only $7,900 was donated by whites; the remaining funds were either raised by Burroughs herself or secured by the Women's Auxiliary. Burroughs once confided, "I've felt that if we colored people could start it and prove that it is worthwhile and would do our very best for it, that before I am clean worn out and can't do any more, He would put it into the heart of some rich white children to do what we can't—endow it and make it a permanent help to my people and my country after I'm dead and gone" (Hammond 1922, 61).

Understanding the majority of her students came from lower-income black families, Burroughs believed the working-class African American could change the black racial profile in the United States. By training students to serve in the best capacity that they could, Nannie believed students would be self-sufficient and highly employable even if the job entailed the lower levels of service. Aiming to professionalize domestic service, Nannie fervently upheld that quality work equates to better pay.

Such a stance positioned Burroughs as a forerunner to advocating equal rights for women. Burroughs gained political prominence as a speaker for African-American women's right to vote and for her advocation of antilynching laws.

With so many African-American women migrating to Washington to seek domestic and civil service jobs, many believed Burroughs was doing more harm than good by providing a curriculum emphasizing domestic service. Some male members of the National Baptists Convention did not support the school, saying Burroughs's education of women to be family breadwinners minimized the role of men in early-twentieth-century society. However, Burroughs rationalized that a NTSGW education in domestic science actually prepared girls for household management and their roles as housewives if not economic stability for families. Burroughs retorted that black males should stop making slaves of black women. Even a 1924 newspaper editorial supported the educational mission of NTSGW, noting, "Nannie Burroughs does not prepare girls for servants, but for service" (Taylor 2002).

Nannie considered herself as much a servant of God as an educator of girls. Aside from women who could be economically self-supporting black women, Nannie sought to educate girls to conduct missionary work, be that as Bible teachers or foreign missionaries. She once told a *Philadelphia Tribune* reporter, "How thankful I am that you think so much of the work that I am trying to do, but my dear sir, I am not among the race's immortals, rather I am just beginning to get my work under way" (Taylor 2002). Among the swelling number of African-American women coming to Washington during World War II, the majority were between the ages of thirteen and thirty and were feared as naive and susceptible to crime and immorality. In this capacity NTSGW served as a refuge for girls from being possible victims of crime, if not moral models of comportment. Nonetheless, Burroughs emphatically reiterated that NTSGW was not a reform school.

Growing enrollment required a constant need for fund-raising efforts by Nannie and her proprietors. The school raised funds by operating a laundry, making and selling goods, and producing and performing in pageants. Other fund-raising projects included recitations, plays, and speaker seminars. Faculty and students sponsored business and professional men's night, young people's night, churches and social welfare organization night, and even a concert that President Calvin Coolidge and his wife, Grace, attended in 1928. All of these events not only raised money for the school but also gave students opportunities at public speaking and entrepreneurship. Burroughs offered her students a more proactive role in public life, which sought to break down the negative images of African-American women in white society.

There was no better example of NTSGW breaking down racial stereotyping of early-twentieth-century African-American women than Bettie B. Reed. When a white family hired Reed to accompany them to their summer home in Maine, the family refused to let Reed use the one bathtub in the home. Reed refused to take the job unless the family relented. The family eventually agreed to Reed's demands, and when they returned in the fall, the family told Burroughs they wanted Reed back with them the following year as well. "She is a great deal cleaner than we are and just as refined. We are sorry we mentioned the bath tub [*sic*]. Our objection was based on mere hearsay about colored people" (Wolcott 1997).

Nannie Burroughs may have served as a flag bearer for black entrepreneurship. As if being principal of the NTSGW was not enough responsibility, Nannie was a member of the National Association of Colored Women and the National League of Republican Colored Women. She formed and served as president for the National Association of Wage Earners to address labor interest and reform for black women in the 1920s. She worked with civil rights activist Harry Haywood to advance the black working class, but stopped as far as promoting his Communist agenda. Burroughs contended that professionally trained women should garner a positive public respect both as a group and as a race.

Graduates of NTSGW reside in all parts of the United States, Puerto Rico, Haiti, and South America. Competence and dependability are attributes often described for the many NTSGW doctors, civil servants, entrepreneurs, social workers, and beauticians who were graduates of the school. In 1959 Burroughs was awarded an honor-roll plaque for her distinguished public service by the *Afro-American* newspaper.

Burroughs died of natural causes at age eighty-two in May 1961. It was estimated that more than five thousand people attended her funeral at the Nineteenth Street Baptist Church in Washington, D.C. Three years later the school was renamed the Nannie Helen Burroughs School. One can only wonder what would have happened had Nannie Helen Burroughs not taken her idea and funds from Louisville's Women's Auxiliary to start her school. There is little doubt that the force of Nannie Helen Burroughs helped change the political, economic, and educational landscape of the United States.

Laura Clay

(1849–1941)

FIRST FEMALE DEMOCRATIC NOMINEE FOR US PRESIDENT; FIRST FEMALE DELEGATE TO THE EPISCOPAL SYNOD

After the day session of the 1920 Democratic National Convention ended at 5:00 p.m. and before the convention reconvened at 8:00 p.m., party leaders attempted to reach a compromise on presidential and vice-presidential candidates during dinner. Each side hoped the other side would give up first, but the balloting deadlock rested on the shoulders of the committee chairs choosing their presidential and vice-presidential candidates. The three leading candidates (Governor James Cox, Secretary of the Treasury W. G. McAdoo, and Attorney General Mitchell Palmer) were each vying for the party platform, yet none was willing to concede his candidacy. The Cox and McAdoo camps presented their presidential and vice-presidential platforms but couldn't secure enough votes. Governor Cox had the majority of votes but not the required two-thirds votes to win nomination.

All three men were wrestling votes from any and all delegates. By the thirtieth ballot, McAdoo was ahead of Cox but sorely needed the big-city bosses' votes. The Indiana delegation threw most of its votes to McAdoo and Cox, but Palmer won Tennessee delegates. Virginia also cast its votes to Palmer by the thirty-fifth ballot. The jockeying began to become exasperating until Kentucky's P. H. Callahan gave a complimentary vote to Laura Clay, whose name was thrown in the ring along with Irvin Cobb and Ring Lardner. Mississippi Senator Pat Harrison moved that the rules be suspended and on each ballot the candidate who received the lowest

Gov. Ruby Laffoon handing gavel to Miss Laura Clay,
temporary chairman of Kentucky convention to
ratify Twenty-first Amendment to the Federal
Constitution, November 27, 1933.

Governor Ruby Laffoon handing a gavel to Laura Clay as Temporary Chairman of the Kentucky Convention to ratify the Twenty-first Amendment to the Constitution (November 7, 1933) The University of Kentucky Photographic Archives

number of votes would be dropped, continuing this practice until the nominee was chosen. Laura Clay received one vote on the thirty-sixth ballot.

Laura Clay must have beamed with pride after being nominated as the first female Democratic nominee for president, topping off an arduous political career. Born on a Madison County, Kentucky, farm in 1849, Laura was the eighth child of General Cassius Clay, cousin of Kentucky famed orator Henry Clay, and Mary Jane Warfield. Her father was the publisher of the emancipationist newspaper the *True American* and a personal friend of Abraham Lincoln. Typical for well-to-do girls, Laura attended finishing school in Lexington and New York. She took classes at both the University of Michigan and the University of Kentucky but seemed unsure about what she wanted to do with her life. When General Clay was appointed ambassador to Russia by Lincoln in 1861, twelve-year-old Laura spent a year in Russia. She watched European women vote and work the jobs their husbands left behind when they went off to war. Such day-to-day activities left an impression on Laura, who had developed an interest in careers in teaching and law.

Laura Clay's true calling to the plight of women's rights occurred when her parents separated and then divorced in 1878. Her own mother had managed to raise ten children, build a $30,000 home (named Whitehall) on a 2,250-acre farm, as well as pay off her husband's 1855 banking debt during his absence while serving his appointment. After her divorce Mary Jane Clay was forced to leave Whitehall, exemplifying the fact that state laws did not protect a woman's legal and property rights. Kentucky allowed a wife's wages to be collected by her husband, and her husband was sole guardian of their children. As late as 1888 Kentucky was the only state that did not permit a married woman to make a will.

It could have been her father's strong antislavery views that triggered Laura's interest in equal rights for all. She wrote in her diary in 1874 that antislavery had taught her "to hate oppression and injustice, and our own domestic life has left my eyes unblinded to the unjust relations between men and women, and the unworthy position of women." Laura's older sister, Mary Clay Herrick, had introduced her to the suffrage movement after Mary attended the founding convention of Lucy Stone's American Woman Suffrage Association in 1869. In 1881 Laura assumed the presidency of the Kentucky Woman Suffrage Association and held that position for twenty-four years, including its reorganization as the Kentucky Equal Rights Association (KERA) in 1888. Laura took over her sister Anne's editorial duties on women's activities for the Lexington *Kentucky Gazette* the same year as her ascendancy into KERA, finding herself the voice and ears of the suffrage movement.

Starting at the local level, KERA spread its agenda through speaking engagements at county fairs and presented contests for the best essays on women's suffrage. The organization got its message out to the public through flyers, pamphlets, and editorial columns in local newspapers. KERA won support from the two largest newspapers in the state, the *Louisville Courier Journal* and the *Lexington Herald.* Laura Clay was influential in coercing legislators to repeal an 1894 statute that restricted school suffrage to women in Lexington, Covington, and Newport. This repeal was passed by the slimmest of margins essentially along party lines. Opponents of the statute believed the legislation gave too many illiterate black women the right to vote. KERA spent its efforts lobbying Frankfort for the protection of married women's property and wages, incorporating female physicians in state female insane asylums, and admission of women into male colleges.

Clay's socially prominent family name offered her access to speak on women's rights at the 1890 Kentucky Constitutional Convention floor, over which her cousin, Henry Clay, presided. In addition to her role in KERA, Laura served as an officer in the Women's Christian Temperance Union, the Kentucky Federation of Women's Club, and the Fayette County ERA. Using her skillful oratory, Laura was able to fold these three organizations' efforts into KERA by advocating legislation that awarded appropriations for a female dormitory at the University of Kentucky, established juvenile courts and detention homes, and raised the age of consent from twelve to sixteen. Clay and her colleagues at KERA were able to increase female appointments to school boards and co-guardianship of children for divorced or separated parents.

Clay's influence within KERA catapulted her name at the national level. In 1895 she was elected the first auditor for the National American Woman Suffrage Association (NAWSA), a post she held for fifteen years, during which membership increased from 17,000 to 45,501. As an unpaid NAWSA field worker, she advanced breakthrough campaigns in Oregon, Oklahoma, and Arizona. Laura Clay and many other suffragists, including her own cousin Madeline McDowell Breckinridge, regularly tapped into their personal wealth to advance many NAWSA causes. Laura Clay subsidized her suffrage work from income she made from her 245-acre farm, which she leased from her father. She even paid the hotel bills for all NAWSA officers attending its national convention in Louisville when the organization was experiencing financial woes in 1911. Two years later NAWSA reported a $1,000 debt owed to Clay. These duties, coupled with her involvement on the membership committee, not only made her a familiar fixture at the local suffragist level but also elevated her as one of the South's most influential suffragists.

While Clay was changing the pendulum for women rights in Kentucky, several southern states began a series of constitutional conventions aimed at disenfranchising African Americans. First in Mississippi in 1890, South Carolina in 1895, and followed by Louisiana in 1898, Democratic, mostly white, political leadership in southern states wanted to maintain political supremacy, even though the black population outnumbered the white population in many southern states. Democratic southern politicians began to believe it might be better to give women the right to vote rather than blacks. The premise behind their reasoning: giving women (albeit white women) the right to vote would tip a greater voting ratio to white voters over black voters. Conversely, the Republican National Committee encouraged black suffrage in a move to break down the Democratic stronghold in the South.

NAWSA needed representation in southern states, so Clay was sent to address the Mississippi (1890), South Carolina (1896), and Louisiana (1898) constitutional conventions. Much like the view held by many of her southern peers, Clay strongly believed white political supremacy for qualified literate voters was a responsible temporary measure until illiterate voters would become educated and then be considered qualified voters. Clay wrote that measures adopted by South Carolina, which compared to those in Mississippi, "unofficially permitted registration officials to register illiterate whites and exclude all blacks of necessity can only be temporary as they promoted fraud as well as ignorance." She realized denying black representation would never fare well with Congress, but she did advocate that suffrage could be given only to literate women regardless of race. It's possible that her stance on disenfranchising illiterate women voters may or may not have been the reason for her losing her bid for auditor reelection in 1911. More likely, this defeat may have been the result of fallout between southern, western, and eastern NAWSA factions over the move of its headquarters from Ohio to New York, a move Clay believed shifted the organization's officers to the east away from the core work of the movement concentrated in the south.

NAWSA wanted to expand its geographic base, but the controversy over states' rights and voting rights for blacks and the uneducated began to divide the organization. Three persistent factions developed within NAWSA: 1) securing suffrage at the federal level, 2) minimal attention addressed toward the federal suffrage movement, and 3) too much attention was given to the federal amendment and not enough at the state level. Discouraged that voting rights to women were overlooked in the Fifteenth Amendment, NAWSA did not want to disenfranchise black suffrage. Realizing disenfranchising black women voters was not conducive to their long-term goals, NAWSA shifted its efforts from a southern strategy to a western strategy. This was no more evident than in the election of one southerner to the NAWSA board of officers: Sophonisba Breckinridge, who had not lived in the South since 1895 and was an active member in the National Association for the Advancement of Colored People.

However, some northern members sympathized with their southern counterparts over the disenfranchisement of black women voters because they feared an increase of new immigrants in their own voting districts. Clay proposed suffrage for all literate women regardless of race.

Yet through her regional field work, Clay was well aware that there were a disproportionate number of illiterate black women to illiterate white women in the South. Clay believed that in the best interest of suffrage, voting rights should be extended to literate versus illiterate voters. This belief mirrored the vast majority of southern white politicians but starkly contradicted the NAWSA national platform. Firmly believing the South would never support a federal suffrage amendment, Clay feared a federal amendment could threaten state control of voting requirements and elections, an extension of autocracy as witnessed in Germany during this time.

Favoring states' rights over federal amendment, Clay was elected vice-president-at-large and focused her attention on a new organization, the Southern States Woman Suffrage Association (SSWSA), founded to win suffrage through state enactment. Clay viewed SSWSA as an auxiliary of, rather than a rival to, NAWSA, whose activities she continued to support. Hoping to appease both federal and states' rights factions, Clay proposed an alternative bill, the United States Election bill, which would give women the right to vote only for congressional and presidential elections, leaving voter qualifications to state mandate. Snubbed by former NAWSA friends due to her allegiance to states' rights, Clay resigned from NAWSA and spent her efforts openly opposing the federal bill. Her efforts proved fruitless once the Nineteenth Amendment, extending the right to vote regardless of gender, was enacted by Congress in June 1919. When NAWSA changed its name to the League of Women Voters after ratification, Clay refused to join or donate, citing, "Now that we have the same voting power to affect legislation as men I believe that women should join men for improved legislation, and not erect any division between the interests of the sexes" (Wheeler 1993, 190).

Laura Clay shifted her activism into politics. Clay organized the Democratic Women's Club of Kentucky and served as a delegate at the San Francisco Democratic National Convention. A sought-after

Democratic speaker, Clay traversed the state for Al Smith during the 1928 presidential election, urging voters not to reject him for his Catholicism or opposition to Prohibition. Hoping to get more women to vote, she ran unsuccessfully at age seventy-four for the state Senate in 1923. She was the Democratic candidate supporting legalization of horse betting, running in a heavily Republican rural district where gambling was considered a sin. Her efforts in women's rights often shifted between politics and religion. She successfully amended the Lexington Episcopal diocese to give women vestry and synod eligibility, culminating in being elected as the first female delegate to the Episcopal Synod in the district of Sewanee in 1924. She waged a campaign for the admission of women to diocesan councils and to the University of the South. At age eighty-six she vocally opposed a plan to pay male teachers more than females as a means of attracting more men into public school teaching positions. Although her public persona was prolific, she enjoyed long hours of bridge and a small circle of friends back in Lexington.

Laura Clay died in 1941 at age ninety-two. Her seven thousand personal papers and other items are housed at the University of Kentucky.

Mary Breckinridge

(1881–1965)

FOUNDER OF THE FIRST MIDWIFERY SERVICE IN THE UNITED STATES

Hyden Hospital needed whiskey and brandy (and lots of it) and milk. Alcohol was often prescribed for pneumonia cases before antibiotics came into existence. Mary Breckinridge, Hyden Hospital's founder, needed government-issued permits to obtain alcohol during Prohibition. Transporting alcohol to Hyden Hospital had potential risks in these parts of the country. Federal agents refused the Frontier Nursing Service's request to ship to the hospital's wholesale drug warehouse. Instead, authorities required alcohol to be shipped in government-bonded packaging to a post office in Hazard, thirteen miles away and teeming with bootleggers. Bootleggers networked throughout the United States during Prohibition but enjoyed a rigorous enterprise among illicit distilleries in this region.

Practicing nursing in the Appalachian foothills had its share of occupational hazards for Mary Breckinridge, notwithstanding the supply chain management. A five- to six-hour horseback ride fording creeks and gaps, little if any toilet facilities, lodging wherever and whenever the sun set, all for payment as little as fifty cents for one's service, was a typical day for Mary Breckinridge. Nonetheless, Mary knew the region's residents lacked a single licensed physician to offer skilled medical care. Local "granny women" cared for pregnant women and young children, often dispensing dangerous medical advice. Since Breckinridge's return from managing a visiting-nurses program in Europe in 1925, she envisioned a nursing program designed to care for women and children from birth to age six.

Mary Breckinridge University of Louisville Photographic Archives

Nursing was not a chosen career path for Mary Breckinridge. Born in Memphis, Tennessee, on February 16, 1881, Mary was the daughter of Clifton Breckinridge, the US ambassador to the court of Czar Nicholas II of Russia. Her grandfather, John Cabell Breckinridge, served as vice president under President James Buchanan. Sophonisba Breckinridge was a distant cousin. She spent several formative years in Europe with her family, tutored by French and German governesses, gaining an appreciation for the finer things in life. Like most young privileged girls, she expected to settle down, marry, and raise her children in comfort.

Life couldn't have been sweeter for Mary after she married her professed soul mate, Henry Morrison, in 1904. However, Henry died just two years later, leaving his twenty-six-year-old widow wondering what to do next. Professions available for unmarried women in those days were mostly limited to teaching and nursing. Although lacking a high school diploma, she poured her grief into nursing studies at St. Luke's Hospital in New York. Returning to Arkansas, where she had lived as a child, she married again, this time bearing two children, a boy and a girl. However, tragedy struck again when her infant daughter died shortly after birth in 1914. Her only surviving child, Breckie, mysteriously died from a brief illness at the age of four two years later. The weight of those two tragedies couldn't sustain Breckinridge's marriage.

Divorce and her two children's deaths propelled Mary to return to nursing. She traveled to Washington, D.C., slums to assist influenza pandemic victims in 1918. Determined to do something that would benefit children, she went to France and worked for the American Red Cross there. The Comité Américain pour les Régions Dévastées de la France (CARDS) provided a visiting nursing program for those rural regions of France impacted by World War I. A resourceful administrator, Mary trained nurses and midwives who would travel throughout the country caring for young French children and pregnant women. Upon her return to the states in 1921, Mary vowed to establish a school for midwifery in the United States.

However, she needed more professional training, so she entered the Teachers College of Columbia University in New York in 1922 to begin studies in public-health nursing. The following summer she conducted a public-health survey, trekking a 650-mile radius among Leslie, Owsley, and Knott Counties in Kentucky's Appalachian Mountains. She compiled a report based on her interviews with lay midwives and local doctors. One of her assistants submitted the findings as a dissertation to Columbia University, proving academic merit to the lack of medical care in the region. The researchers learned most births were assisted by local women, dubbed "granny women," who were illiterate and unskilled in nursing. Lacking a licensed physician, the region had the highest birth and infant mortality rates in the country. Moreover, the area suffered from the highest death rate for women in childbirth in the developing world.

After completing her studies at Columbia University, Mary traveled to England and enrolled in London's British Hospital for Mothers and Babies. In England, professional nurses were trained as midwives, contrary to training in the United States. It made sense to Mary that nurses trained in midwifery could have a significant impact on the health care of children living in rural America. However, a national debate ensued regarding whether or not problems would occur if midwives replaced obstetricians. The controversy centered on the belief that high fees (at the time three times higher than midwives) charged by obstetricians would make it difficult to replace midwives. Given that obstetricians tended to practice near urban areas, it was believed those areas might see a downtrend in quality maternity care. On the flip side, obstetricians worked autonomously, thus being more difficult to regulate than midwives.

The approach to the childbirth process differed significantly between midwives and obstetricians of the time. Midwives were unwilling to intervene in the natural childbirth process. In fact, midwives advocated a change in the birthing practice from the supine to upright position. Obstetricians, in contrast, highlighted the dangers that arose during pregnancy and childbirth and thus trained in intervention should the situation require it. During a 1925 White House conference, it was reported that forceps were being used in 10 to 80 percent of births across the United States. This contrasted to 4 percent of births in Scandinavian countries, where midwives attended more than 80 percent of births. Mary could attest to the research that confirmed that when midwifery declined, the incidence of maternal mortality and infant birth mortality rose. During the 1920s this pattern was evident in both Cleveland, Ohio, and Newark, New Jersey.

Armed with her certification in midwifery, Breckinridge began a yearlong study of the Highlands and Islands Medical and Nursing Service, which served the rough country of northern Scotland and islands off its western shore. Her tenure in Scotland proved useful, and when Mary returned to Leslie County, Kentucky, in 1925, she instituted the Kentucky Committee for Mothers & Babies. Surprised she was able to recruit interest to her mission, Mary pulled together a committee of prominent citizens that included eight doctors, the presidents of Berea College and the University of Kentucky, a newspaper editor, an officer with the Louisville & Nashville Railroad, several well-respected mountain workers, and a gubernatorial candidate. Aside from key civic leaders, Mary also solicited financial support from fraternal organizations such as the Kentucky Federation of Women's Club based in Louisville and the Kentucky Women's Club in New York.

Renamed the Frontier Nursing Service (FNS) in 1928, Kentucky Committee for Mothers & Babies opened in Hyden, Kentucky, in a nondescript two-story building with a small medical dispensary serving as headquarters. The ruggedness and remoteness of the Scottish Highlands mirrored Kentucky's Appalachian Mountains not only in topography but also in economic and social circumstances. Mary planned to emulate the Scottish version of the organization, which set up nursing districts staffed with qualified nurses dispersed evenly throughout the region. In areas with several nursing centers, a medical center would be located and staffed with a physician trained in obstetrics and gynecology and two nurse-midwives. Nurses would have paid salaries; fees for services would be established by local committees based on the local economy.

Kentucky and the Scottish Highlands also shared the trait of unfailing familial solidarity. Choosing Kentucky to establish the Frontier Nursing Service seemed feasible since Mary Breckinridge could tap into the financial resources and public awareness of her family name. When the chairman of a mountaineer rally to build a nursing center introduced Mary, he explained that her people held "high office" in the state and not one of them had betrayed a public trust. On Christmas Day 1925, Mary wanted to get to know the neighbors as well as promote public awareness for the service. She invited all ten thousand residents of Leslie County to a Christmas party at her unfinished home. Although only five hundred showed up, Mary served free food, and her wealthy friends sent gifts for the children, many of whom barely had food on their own tables much less Christmas presents. The party was a success and continues to be an annual yuletide tradition.

Initially, six British-trained midwives, working in pairs, traversed the region tending to prenatal care and assorted ailments ranging from diarrhea to typhoid. Nurses spent forty hours a week working in clinics, then made visits to expectant mothers. Maternity patients were seen every two weeks until the seventh month, then weekly after the seventh month. At a moment's notice a nurse was required to go since Breckinridge believed a nurse's presence at the onset of labor had ramifications on delivery. After delivery a nurse provided daily care for the first ten days of infancy, then twice a month until lactation was successful. In one year alone, 1951, FNS nurses assisted in more than 8,596 deliveries. By 1989, those numbers more than doubled. FNS nurses assisted in a staggering 22,477 births with only eleven maternal deaths.

Because there were only four indoor toilets in Leslie County, the greatest public health problems the nurses tended to were tuberculosis, trachoma (a viral eye disease), and intestinal worms. Two bathtubs were reported in the whole region. Poor sanitation contributed to the prevalence of hookworms, which afflicted more than one-third of children, and roundworm was found in nine out of ten children. Severe cases were sent to either Lexington or Louisville for medical, surgical, or hospital inpatient care. Eight hundred twenty Hyden children participated in a Vanderbilt and Johns Hopkins Universities study for a new drug, hexylresorcinol, to rid intestinal parasites. FNS nurses' records were instrumental for local county public service agencies to keep abreast of community medical needs.

Not only did the FNS nurses need to establish a rapport with their patients, they needed to be cautious of pseudo doctors, or untrained physicians, armed with medical staples such as syringes but without board-certified medical degrees. One particular disturbing couple Breckinridge encountered looked rather proper and intelligent. However, the husband had acquired his healing skills through on-the-job practice, while his wife, a lay midwife, wielded a hypodermic needle filled with pituitrin (a coagulant used for preventing postpartum hemorrhaging) rather than Pitocin to hasten labor. Frontier nurses were successful in circumventing such characters, and a testament to this was their success serving rural families within a seven-hundred-mile area. When circumstances turned dire a nurse would turn to the *Medical Routine* manual written by physicians who served on the FNS's medical advisory committee. The *Medical Routine* manual walked nurses through emergency scenarios in which narcotics such as morphine or codeine were necessary outside the presence of a licensed doctor. Breckinridge often cited the manual as evidence against those who accused her nurses of dispensing illegal drugs.

By 1928 private donations financed the building of the twenty-five-bed, twelve-bassinet Hyden Hospital and the hiring of its first medical director. By 1933 the hospital and physicians supported eleven district nursing centers throughout the region. Such expansion efforts, in addition to the expense of sending American nurses to England for midwife training, prompted Breckinridge to establish the Frontier School of Midwifery and Family Nursing, the first of its kind in the United States. Midwifery training consisted of a six-month program of classroom instruction and field work. Breckinridge understood that formal training not only gave nurses professional standing among their medical counterparts, but also gave female nurses professional autonomy to withstand fluctuations in economic instability. For the next thirty years, Breckinridge managed to raise more than $6 million to support and enlarge FNS. The organization became the backbone for the inception of the American Association of Nurse-Midwives in 1929.

This professionalization of midwifery in the United States was not without its detractors. For example, an editorial in the *West Virginia Medical Journal* harshly criticized a 1925 bill authorizing the training and licensing of midwives and stated it was "thoroughly disgusted with its operation" (Barney 2000, 136). Regional doctors encouraged the FNS service in rural eastern Kentucky, but many were suspect of its use in urban communities. Mountaineer women were hesitant to spend $10 for a midwife delivery that their own mothers had not found necessary.

Suffering from bladder cancer and leukemia, Mary Breckinridge died at age eighty-four on May 16, 1965. Outfitted in her riding uniform and with pictures of her two children and locks of their hair, she was buried next to them in a Lexington cemetery. In her forty years of service with the FNS, Mary Breckinridge tended to more than fifty thousand registered patients and administered a quarter of a million inoculations. She bequeathed the organization $2 million after her death. Today the school is considered the longest continually operating nurse-midwifery program in the nation. It met its goal of lowering the maternal mortality rate in Leslie County, and it still serves southeastern Kentucky. In June 2007 fifty-five students from Georgia, Texas, Massachusetts, Utah, and beyond gathered on the steep hillside near the barn where the horses used to be stabled, prepared to start classes at the Frontier graduate program. The *U.S. News and World Report* lists the Frontier School as the forty-seventh-best graduate nursing program in the country out of seventy-two.

Aunt Molly Jackson

(1880–1960)

FOLK SINGER FOR UNION ACTIVISM

Aunt Molly Jackson, armed with a 38 special—which was a constant companion during her travels around the mountain region—walked to the county commissary with her son Henry. She ordered a bag of flour for two famished coal families, gave it to Henry, and told him to go wait by the coal tipple outside. She approached the counter and told the clerk to credit the $5.90 to her account. The commissary clerk told her no way. With that Aunt Molly pulled out her gun and gingerly walked back toward the door as she replied, "Martin, if you try to take this grub away from me, God knows if they electrocute me for it tomorrow, I'll shoot you six times a minute. I've got to feed some children; they're hungry and can't wait." She walked out the door.

Although she made it home, she was eventually greeted by the deputy sheriff, summoning her arrest. When asked if she was a robber, Aunt Molly retorted, "I'm no robber, but I said, hit [*sic*] was the last chance, I have heard these little hungry children cry for something to eat 'til I'm desperate; I'm almost out of my mind . . . you know I am as honest as the day is long. . . ." Upon hearing her plea, the deputy sheriff was unable to carry out the coal operator's wish to arrest her. The deputy sheriff said to Aunt Molly, "If you have the heart to do that much . . . for other's people's children that not's got one drap [*sic*] of blood in their bodies, I will pay that bill myself and . . . if they fire me for not arresting you, I will be damned glad of it" (Martin 2002, 471). He walked off never having handcuffed Aunt Molly.

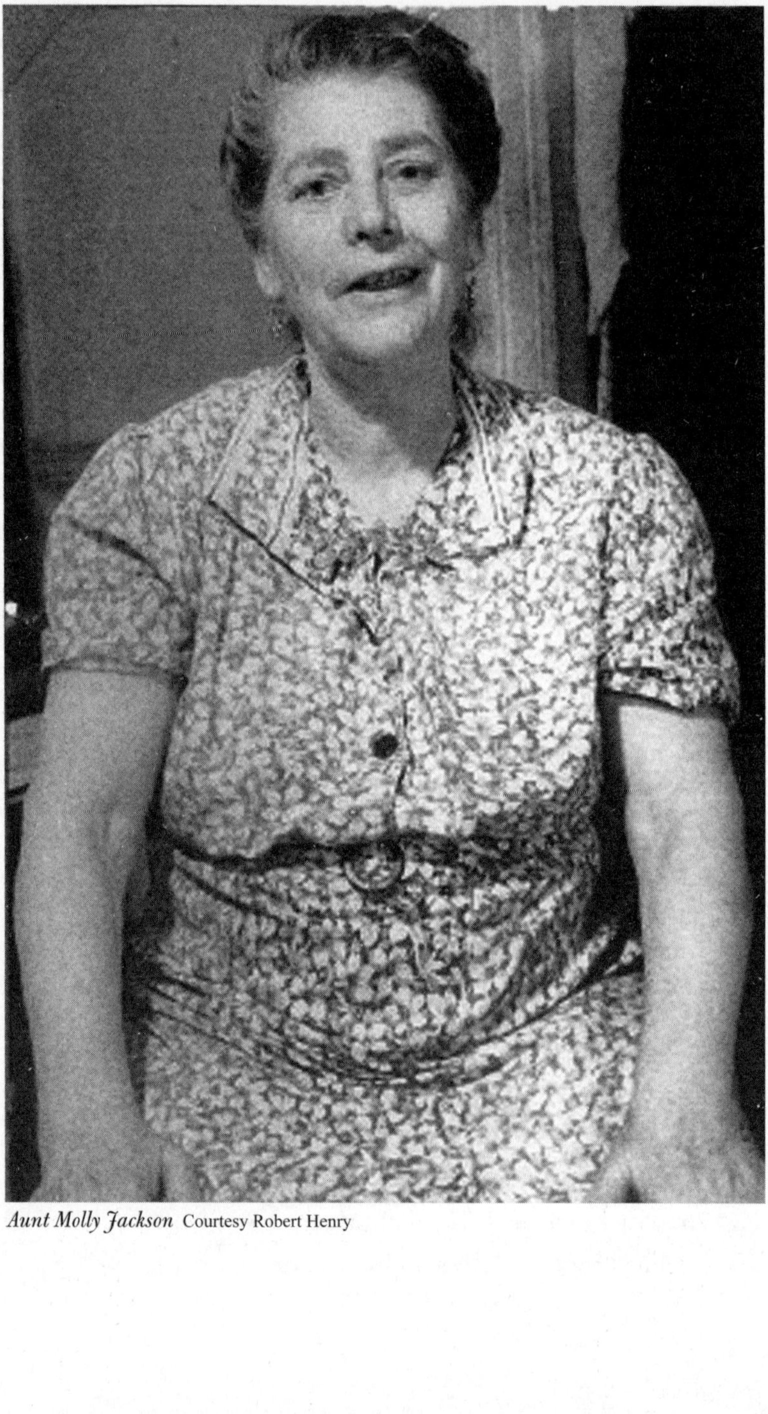

Aunt Molly Jackson Courtesy Robert Henry

Awareness for the marginalized pockets of society was instilled in Aunt Molly Jackson by her miner-preacher father. Affectionately known as Aunt Molly, Mary Magdalene Garland was born in 1880 in Clay County the oldest child of Oliver and Deborah Robinson Garland. Clay County was home to the Garland and Robinson families for seven generations, starting with the first Garland arriving in the region in 1637. Oliver farmed, worked in the coal mines, and was a Baptist minister. When her mother and sister died within six weeks of each other, six-year-old Molly Garland became a fill-in mother to her four younger siblings. She said, "The death of my little sister and the death of my mother is the first sorrow I ever knew, since then God only knows all the sadness and sorrow I have lived through" (Martin 2002, 470). Molly understood from an early age the marriage between struggling coal-mining families and abject poverty.

When her father remarried within a year of her mother's death, her career path was all but chosen for her: nursing and midwifery. By the time Molly turned nine, she was a nursemaid to two of her stepsiblings and helped maintain a growing household, which eventually totaled fourteen children. In between her household duties, she accompanied her father to union meetings and served her first jail sentence by age ten. Her jail sentence was not for social injustice but for a prank gone wrong: she blackfaced herself, grabbed her grandfather's rifle, and tried to frighten a few neighborhood children.

By age fourteen she married miner Jim Stewart and bore two sons, both victims of childbirth complications. Raising Jim's two children from a previous relationship, she and Jim would relocate among coal camps dotting along the region. Jim worked the coal mines while Molly nursed and practiced midwifery. In between, the two attended a Clay County moonlight school. Moonlight schools originated in Rowan County, Kentucky, in 1911 to provide basic reading and writing skills to individuals who did not have the advantage to attend public schools. The classes were held at night because the surrounding counties were still known to be wracked with feuds. Local feuding coupled with the lack of modern electricity prompted most residents not to venture out at night. The moon would "light" the way for students on their way to class. The students who attended moonlight schools ranged from adult men who dropped out of school at an early age and saw the disadvantage of not being able to read to women with babies in tow who desired to read the family Bible.

Although Molly's skill was bringing life into the world, odds were against her being successful at it. By the early 1900s many states began outlawing midwifery. For mountain women without access to hospitals, midwifery was the only medical care a pregnant woman could seek. In fact, a competent midwife was an asset for mountain women. Molly once guessed she had probably attended five thousand births over the course of her midwifery career. It was reported that Aunt Molly delivered at least 884 babies between Clay and Harlan Counties alone. She became a certified midwife by age eighteen. If she had carried any resentment for helping to raise her stepsiblings, Aunt Molly seemed to overcome any such bitterness by becoming a skilled and much-sought-after midwife. She and her second husband continued to travel from coal camp to coal camp tending the sick and wounded or delivering babies. Her Hippocratic oath stemmed from the New Testament: "Treat every human being as one would want to be treated."

Life working in coal mines dealt families a cruel blow and Molly suffered the same tragedies as anyone else. In 1917 Jim was killed in a mine by a rock fall. Her father suffered optic nerve damage after being struck by falling slate. One of her brothers was crushed by a boulder. One of her sons was struck and killed by a slate slide. This plus the fact that coal company owners failed to extend profits to their suffering workers prompted Molly to turn to song as a psychological release amid union struggles and poverty conditions.

Following Jim Stewart's death, Molly married another miner, Bill Jackson. Bill Jackson and his brother operated a still deep in the Appalachian Mountains. Carrying a pistol for protection, Molly rode out one weekend to bring the pair back home. As she came upon the still, she called out, "Bill Jackson, you come down heah now," to which he replied, "Now Mame I ain't comin' down till you lay that pistol down" (Aunt Molly Jackson . . . "Original 'Pistol Packin' Mama'" 1960). Jackson's brother wrote this exchange into a rough verse for the song "Pistol Packin' Mama" by Tin Pan Alley, which became an instant hit.

Molly's personality belied a strong-willed woman who could handle the harsh realism of the marginalized coal community. Aunt Molly joined many of her fellow mountain women not only to build morale for coal miners but actually to organize and participate in union strikes. When the coal strikes became incensed during the late 1920s and early 1930s, Aunt Molly participated with other southern Appalachian women in wildcat strikes. Her role as a midwife required her to travel in and among eastern Kentucky's mountain region rallying strikers with speeches and ballads.

Her brother, Jim Garland, recalled an incident when a group of scabs and gun thugs approached a picket line set up by local women. The women manhandled the thugs and stripped them naked while the men took off through a cornfield after the strikebreakers. After four men held one of the gun thugs, Aunt Molly took his pistol and shoved the barrel right into his rectum. Needless to say, the man was never seen again. She became known as the "pistol-packing mama."

Aunt Molly was one of the witnesses interviewed by the National Committee for the Defense of Political Prisoners in late 1931. The twelve-member committee, mostly comprised of distinguished leftist writers, was founded a few months earlier as an adjunct to the International Labor Defense (ILD), which was led by the Communist party. One of its organizers, novelist Theodore Dreiser, summed up the committee's mission as one in which American intellectuals would stand up for the American worker and aid workers to defend themselves against terror and suppression.

Some committee members came to Harlan County to investigate the abuse presented in a thirty-two-page indictment against the coal operators by the ILD. Jackson relayed to writers John Dos Passos and Dreiser the pervasive starvation and groundswell of violence during the coal strikes. Aunt Molly told the men of the bad conditions of housing and food within coal camps. She recounted how coal company doctors refused to come to the aid of a coal miner's family unless they were paid in advance. In those circumstances, Molly had to nurse starving children until the children took their last breaths. Thirty-seven children died in her arms during a three-month period in 1931.

So it was not fame and fortune that Aunt Molly pursued but political inspiration that was characteristic of the mountain culture. She fervently believed her songs should be inspiring for working people. The final straw of despair came after Molly witnessed her own half-sister Sarah Ogan Gunning's fourteen-month-old baby die from starvation while the coal operators dressed in finery. The tragedy inspired her to write her famous song "I am a Union Woman" in 1931, followed by "Kentucky Miner's Wife" and "Poor Miner's Farewell."

She performed her renditions before the National Committee for the Defense of Political Prisoners. Theodore Dreiser, Sherwood Anderson, Lewis Mumford, and Waldo Frank all persuaded Molly to go north, suggesting she tour the country to promote relief for the miners. The choice to leave Kentucky was fairly obvious for Molly given she was blacklisted in the mining community. She and her brother performed before twenty-one thousand at the New York Coliseum and helped raise $900 for striking miners. An instant hit, Molly's ballad "Kentucky Miners Hungry Blues" charmed audiences with opening stanzas such as:

I am sad and wearied; I have got the hungry, ragged blues,
Not a penny in my pocket to buy one thing I need to use.
I was up in this morning with the worst blues I ever had in my life.
Not a bite to cook for breakfast, or for a coal miner's wife.

With the Depression in full swing, such lyrics resonated with audiences around the country.

By the end of 1935, Aunt Molly and Jim Garland teamed with her half-sister. The trio performed with Pete Seeger, Woody Guthrie, and Leadbelly (Huddie Ledbetter), infusing folk music into a political torch song. Aunt Molly's ebullient spirit impressed Leadbelly so much that he wrote a song about her:

Aunt Molly Jackson
It gives me great satisfaction
To work with Aunt Molly Jackson.
She walks, she talks, she fights.
She unites the working class.

Aunt Molly settled in New York's Lower East Side, not in a much better socioeconomic stature than what she left in Kentucky's Appalachian Mountains, appearing in politically left rallies. Her association with IDL eventually typecast her as a socialist and Communist. She retorted, "I've been framed up and accused of being a Red when I did not understand what they meant. I never heard tell of a Communist until I left Kentucky—then I had passed fifty—but they called me a Red. I got all of my progressive ideas from my hard struggles, and nowhere else" (Martin 2002). Not everyone back in Kentucky was pleased by Molly's activism. Bill Jackson divorced her in 1931 to escape reprisal from her union activity and his battle with unemployment.

Her divorce was just one highlight in 1931. She also recorded her first commercial record, *Kentucky Miner's Wife: Ragged Hungry Blues,* for Columbia Records in the same studio and the same month as notable artists Guy Lombardo and His Royal Canadians, Kate Smith, and the Dorsey Brothers. Aunt Molly influenced a group of radical composers—including Charles Seeger, Aaron Copland, and Marc Blitzstein—to organize the Composers Collective in 1932. The Composers Collective was a left-wing musicians' workshop that created and re-created folk songs as an organizing, if not propagandist, tool for change in class struggle. Many of its members were classically trained composers from conservatories at Harvard, Juilliard, and Columbia.

However, her good fortune seemed to run out. During one of her stints traveling through Ohio, she was involved in a bus accident that left her briefly incapacitated. She became disenchanted with Columbia Records (believing they shortchanged her by 15 percent). By the early 1940s Aunt Molly became more a symbol of the Communist left than a songstress, and thus her audiences started to shrink during the Communist Red Scare of the 1950s. She attempted to pen a labor song book but could not attract a publisher. Feeling exploited and depressed, she and her third husband moved to the West Coast in 1943. Up until her death in 1960, she steadfastly held to the authenticity of her text in the same manner as she held to the union activism of her earlier days. The recordings of Aunt Molly Jackson, author of more than one hundred folk songs, are now housed in the Library of Congress. Not bad for a coal miner's daughter from eastern Kentucky.

Laura Miller Derry

(1905–1993)

FIRST CIVILIAN FEMALE ATTORNEY TO WIN AN ARMY COURT-MARTIAL

"Private Finn, this court finds you not guilty. . . ." Laura Miller Derry's exhilaration was palpable when the announcement came that her client, Private Walter H. Finn, thirty-three, had been acquitted of a rape charge. She could hardly concentrate on the remainder of the verdict at the end of the three-day court-martial at Fort Knox. "The longest twenty-five minutes in my life was while the jury, I mean members, were out considering the verdict," Laura told reporters (Porter 1944, 16). As the first civilian female attorney to successfully win a court-martial, Derry knew the stakes were high for her client: acquittal, the death penalty, or life imprisonment, the Army way.

Initially she hesitated to take the case, knowing Army court-martials do not have a reputation for leniency, with rape being the most difficult to defend, but she was approached by Private Finn's wife to take on the case. Balancing the responsibility of the case against the Army private's life and family, she dropped most of her other legal duties and immersed herself in the *Court-Martial Practical Guide* and *A Manual for Court-Martial, U.S. Army*. The differences between civil and military trials were evident. Military trial protocol determines who sits by whom in the courtroom. There were no trick questions or browbeating the witness. All eleven members sitting on the court-martial were permitted to ask questions—and did—of any of the witnesses.

Making strides in the legal profession was not necessarily what Laura Miller Derry set out to do. Born in 1905 in Horse Cave, Kentucky, Derry learned everything from raising chickens to making pies but

Laura Miller Derry by Al Blunk, the Louisville Courier-Journal, *June 22, 1949*

The *Louisville Courier-Journal*

didn't really excel at anything. After learning shorthand she spent three years typing railroad freight bills and tickets, allowing her to travel extensively throughout the United States. During this period she spent time sightseeing in New Orleans at Mardi Gras and museums in New York, wrapping up her travels with a round-trip covering Colorado, Hollywood, Seattle, Alaska, and Chicago. Although the travel was exciting for a twenty-two-year-old, Laura decided it was time to choose a career.

She got a job working as a nurse and typist in Los Angeles, taking nighttime short-story classes in Hollywood. Laura hopped between jobs as a sound engineer for a movie studio and an administrative assistant for the Red Cross. Her railroad pass was soon to expire so she took job teaching shorthand at a business college in Newark, New Jersey. Hoping to land a teaching position at $125 a month, she took night classes at New Jersey State Teachers College and Rutgers University. When the Depression hit, the business college was forced to let her go from her teaching job, so she took her college credits and returned to Bowling Green, Kentucky.

By 1933 Derry received a bachelor's degree in commercial education from Bowling Green College of Commerce. The financially struggling graduate took a job managing the county newspaper for $75 a month. Over the course of two years, she worked as a political campaigner and cub reporter/editor, but realized very little of her pay was going into her own pocket. So, Derry enrolled in law school, attending classes while working two jobs at the Louisville Convention and Public League and in the research department for the City of Louisville.

Three years later Derry graduated with high honors from Jefferson School of Law with her LL.B., one of five women in a class of 126. After her admission to the Kentucky Court of Appeals, she was introduced to the assistant attorney general and began practicing law within the Jefferson County circuit courts. With the Depression at its peak, Derry had no money to start a law practice so she returned to teaching high school history and business education. She opened her law practice after classes ended. Her perseverance paid off after her admittance to practice before the Veterans Administration (1938), the United States Supreme Court (1941), and the US Court of Military Appeals (1956).

With World War II in its early campaigns, it was clear that a vacuum existed in the military for manufacturing equipment, distribution of equipment, and other administrative tasks. Congresswomen Edith Rouse introduced a bill in the House of Representatives to establish the Women's Army Auxiliary Corps (WAAC). The creation of the WAAC in 1942 offered women the opportunity to serve in a quasi-military function, performing jobs, mostly clerical, that the Army would have otherwise given to enlisted men. As a conduit for enrolling women to fill administrative positions once occupied by men, WAAC was eligible to enroll up to 150,000 officers and enlisted women between the ages of twenty-one and forty-five for noncombatant duty.

Women lawyers often served as WAAC officers and, by the end of the war, more than 150 members of the National Association of Women Lawyers, of which Derry was a member, donned uniforms. Laura Miller Derry had made a name for herself as one of two NAWL national leaders to actively serve in recruiting and public affairs within the WAAC. While participating in the WAAC's Civilian Advisory Committee, Derry assisted with offering free legal service to enlisted men at the Fort Knox Legal Service.

It was during her WAAC legal committee work that she was tapped by Private Finn's wife for his rape trial. The events preceding Finn's trial illustrate irresponsible if not embarrassing behavior. As one of the few servicemen who had a car, Private Finn often transported people in and around the base. One night he accompanied another soldier and the soldier's girlfriend to a tavern near Shively. He picked up a girl and the pair left the other members of the party at the nightclub and rode back to the girl's home in New Albany, Indiana. What behavior carried on between the pair remains to be told, but two days later Finn was detained at the Fort Knox guardhouse and accused of rape after the girl swore in an affidavit against him. Derry secured his acquittal and the trial set a precedent in military law. Finn was probably more than anxious to take his car and head back to work in the family gas station in Berkeley, California.

The rules for an Army court-martial are regulated by the *U.S. Articles of War*. There were three kinds of court-martial during World War II: the summary court, the special court, and the general court. The summary court-martial consists of one commissioned officer who acts as a judge and jury in the trial of a soldier accused of violation of an article of war or minor offense. A special court-martial consists of three commissioned officers who must adjudge a case with two-thirds majority. Any general officer commanding an army, a territorial division, or department or a colonel commanding a separate department may initiate a general court-martial. General court-martials may consist of no fewer than thirteen commissioned officers, unless a number less than thirteen could greatly impact military service. There must be two-thirds majority for a ten-year sentence, three-fourths majority for more than ten years, and a unanimous majority for either life imprisonment or the death penalty.

Upon charges being filed and oaths being sworn, an investigation of witnesses takes place and an Army charge sheet is completed. The charge sheet is the Army's formal indictment and contains, among other information, military demographic information of the accused, witness interviews, evidence, and the specific article being violated to be used by defense counsel and investigating officers. The charge sheet is forwarded to the commanding officer of the unit, who decides whether to hold the court-martial trial in an inferior court (summary or special) or to an investigating officer (general). If the trial goes to general court, then the investigating officer has three main duties: identify the facts of the case, report whether the charges are in proper form, and make a recommendation as to disposition. If the investigating officer recommends trial by general court-martial and the commanding officer concurs, the charge sheet and statements are given to the superior officer who reviews the case (a second review) to determine if the case merits general court-martial. Once the superior officer warrants the case be held in a general court-martial, the case is referred to the trial judge advocate of the general court.

A general court-martial trial allows the accused a right of counsel, either court appointed or personal choice. A swearing in by the court, trial judge advocate, and assistant is taken. Similar to civilian trials, testimony and evidence mandated by the *Manual for Court-Martial U.S. Army* begins for both prosecution and defense. The court closes at the conclusion of prosecution and defense and makes its finding of either guilty or innocent. Once the court reaches one of these findings, it reopens to hear personal data concerning the accused and/or a record of previous conviction by court-martial. The court closes again and then votes on a sentence. Since the entire proceedings are transcribed, the record is forwarded to the appointing authority for the judge advocate that makes the review and recommends action taken by the appointing authority. The procedure must adhere to the final adjudication found in the *Articles of War* 46, 48, and 50.

After the sentence has been confirmed, an order is issued directing punishment to be carried out. This is known as the general court-martial order. Derry noted, "When an offense is brought to trial and the procedure outlined above is followed, there is no miscarriage of justice. Under this system when properly administered, it is practically impossible for an innocent person to be convicted or for an excessive sentence to be inflicted on a guilty person" (Derry 1946).

Dating back to the 1775 Continental Congress, both the Army and Navy had separate military criminal court systems. The *Articles of War* mandated the Army's military criminal system founded on principles of an antiquated military order whereby the commander's duty was to exercise military discipline when and where he deemed appropriate. Subsequently, commanding officers often used the military court to serve their own interest rather than as a means to protect the rights of an accused.

Derry attributed the pervasiveness of military court-martials to two causes. First, investigating personnel were also staff officers who exposed problems of impartiality and inadequate time to thoroughly investigate a charge. Secondly, the investigating officer had a limited time frame to conduct an investigation before bringing the case to court, and many times this amounted to a mere twenty-four hours to build a case. This situation resulted in what Derry called "sandwiching the time of the trial into such hours where all parties are interested in one objective: to conclude the trial as quickly as possible" (Derry 1946). Derry recommended the system create a separate bipartisan branch (without recommendation from a commanding officer or other branch of the Army) to impartially investigate all charges before the start of a trial.

The American public was furious over the revelation that one court-martial case occurred for every eight service members who served in the armed forces during World War II. More than sixty general court-martialed convictions occurred for each day of fighting. Laura Miller Derry wrote in a 1946 *Women Lawyers Journal* article that 60 to 75 percent of court-martial cases tried resulted from errors in the pretrial investigations rather than flaws within the *Manual for Court-Martial U.S. Army*. Derry, then president of the national NAWL, blamed legal shortcomings squarely on military justice officers, not the *Manual for Court-Martial U.S. Army,* which at the time was being labeled "outdated" by the War Department and the press.

She was just one of many influential voices that caused President Harry Truman to sign into law the Uniform Code of Military Justice (UCMJ) in 1950. Congressional hearings after World War II resulted in dramatic changes to the UCMJ10 (USC 831, et seq), marking sweeping changes in military criminal law including the right to counsel and accountability of military duties. For example, Article 31, UCMJ (1951), requires that military personnel suspected of an offense be advised of their right to refuse questioning. Derry was instrumental in outlining postwar plans for returning veterans.

Her 1944 court-martial case may have made national press but she also was an influential figure at the local level. Outside of her famous military trial, she was instrumental in implementing a $40,000 reduction in Louisville water rates. Between spending one hundred hours rolling bandages for the Red Cross, she participated in war bond drives, patriotic radio programs, and local blood drives. She served several years on the mayor of Louisville's legislative committee, Louisville Radio Council, and the Louisville Bar Association's speakers bureau. She earned an honorary doctorate from the University of Louisville in 1950. The culmination of all her military work would have reached its apex when Derry was commissioned an admiral of Cherry River Navy (West Virginia).

On the national level she became an accredited observer to the United Nations in 1946, acting as a representative to the UN Relief and Rehabilitation Council Meeting. Her tenure as a representative on both President Harry Truman's Highway Safety Commission and President Dwight Eisenhower's Occupational Safety Conference gave her opportunities to network with a wider circle of female lawyers. These experiences prompted her to compile and edit the 480-page book *Digest of Women Lawyers and Judges* in 1949, which was often used in both law libraries and high schools as a career reference tool. She conducted a national survey of women in public service in 1956 and a survey of women lawyers in public service in the United States the following year.

A particular high point of her career was her selection by the German embassy as one of seven US attorneys to make a thirty-one-day tour of West Germany in 1957. While traveling continental Europe Derry and her dignitaries were invited to a reception at Buckingham Palace by Queen Elizabeth II. Aside from the amenities of the trip, Derry got right to business in sitting on the arrangements committee for the American bar meeting.

Although she enjoyed the fruits of her travels, Laura was drawn back to Kentucky, either to her Louisville residence or her Leitchfield tobacco farm. She married Major Steven Derry in 1944 and raised a daughter, Portia, during the height of her career. She remained in practice until 1990 and died in 1993 at the age of eighty-seven.

Alice Allison Dunnigan

(1906–1983)

FIRST AFRICAN-AMERICAN FEMALE JOURNALIST TO COVER THE WHITE HOUSE, CONGRESS, SUPREME COURT, AND STATE DEPARTMENT

Alice Dunnigan didn't expect to be accosted by police while traveling in the press corps covering President Harry S. Truman's two-week, nine-thousand-mile tour of the western United States. Who would have thought that Cheyenne, Wyoming, military police would have grabbed her and told her to get behind the crowd barricade even though she walked among sixty journalists behind the presidential motorcade? She wore the three-inch press badge in plain view, but that was to no avail when the soldier grabbed her and pushed her toward the edge of the street. Luckily, a white male reporter came to her rescue, but this was hardly the reception Alice was expecting, especially since she had to obtain a personal loan to pay for the presidential trip since her employer, Associated Negro Press, refused to pay her way.

A few days later Dunnigan was relaxing in her train compartment, typing her daily news feed, when she heard a tap at the door. President Truman walked in. As she struggled with the typewriter in her lap to get up to answer the door, all that could be seen were her bare feet. Dunnigan recalled, "I tugged at my skirt. I couldn't find my shoes. I knew I should be standing up, but I couldn't move." Truman inquired, "I heard you had a little trouble. Well, if anything else happens, please let me know" (Streitmatter 1994, 113). Truman's quiet reassurance was enough to encourage Dunnigan to continue on with the presidential tour, eventually ending the year honored as the first African-American female White House correspondent.

Alice Allison Dunnigan was all too familiar with life setbacks and extenuating circumstances. She always had a purpose to succeed. Born in 1906 in Russellville, Kentucky, she was the granddaughter of slaves. Her father, Willie, was a tenant farmer, and her mother, Lena, a laundress. Taking her mother's lead, Dunnigan learned the laundry business could be used to supplement her income, but she had other aspirations. If she wasn't told by her father that an education was useless for a girl, she was reminded by her mother that she was too unattractive to attract a husband.

However, Alice's strict upbringing fostered her dreams of a life beyond Russellville, and journalism would take her there. Attending school one day a week, she learned to read before first grade. By age thirteen she started writing one-sentence news blurbs about church activities for the black newspaper *Owensboro Enterprise.* She sold copies for five cents but kept three cents for herself. Although the pay was paltry, Alice supplemented her income by tutoring black students, cleaning homes for white people, and washing dishes. Her hard work paid off when she graduated at the top of her high school class and received a personal loan to attend the Kentucky Normal and Industrial Institute (now Kentucky State University) in Frankfort.

After earning her teacher's certificate in 1924, Alice spent the next eighteen years teaching in small one-room schoolhouses. While teaching Kentucky history she realized her students were unaware of the contributions of African Americans to the state's history. She decided to remedy this by creating Kentucky fact sheets, which she used in addition to the assigned textbook. Undeterred, she sent the fact sheets to Frank Stanley, publisher of the *Louisville Leader,* a black city newspaper, who published them in a weekly column. So popular was "The Achievements of the Kentucky Negro" column that the publisher hired Dunnigan as its

Alice Dunnigan, the only woman reporter interviewing Senator Brooks (R-IL) in his office, Senate Office Building (1948) Manuscript, Archives, and Rare Book Library, Emory University

women's editor, writing a column titled "Negro Women's Contribution to American History." She expanded her writing to publishing articles for newspapers in Louisville, Paducah, and Hopkinsville. Although she could not find a publisher for the fact sheets in 1939, forty-three years later, in 1982, Associated Publishers finally published her *Fascinating Story of Black Kentuckians: Their Heritage and Tradition.* The book was compiled from her articles that were published in the *Louisville Defender* and the *Leader.*

Her personal life was unfulfilling and discouraging to her dreams. Alice married her first husband, but discovered after four years of marriage he lacked a respect for education. Her second husband (a childhood friend who fathered her only son, Robert) preferred physical and mental abuse to remind Alice of her duties as a housewife. Her summers were spent doing odd jobs such as washing cemetery tombstones, cleaning homes, washing clothes, and cooking meals for a meager seven dollars a week. When the Depression hit, disadvantaged blacks fared worse than their white counterparts. It was not uncommon for Dunnigan to search the city dump for salvable food for her family while helping to clear an African-American cemetery, which was located next to it. She wrote in her autobiography, "Often we would find such things as cabbage rotten on the outside. We would remove those rotten leaves and carry the cabbage home for cooking" (Dawson 2007, 40).

Outside of her home life, Alice did not shy away from adversity. In 1935 the Works Progress Administration (WPA) was a relief measure that offered work to the unemployed by providing jobs in construction, slum clearance, reforestation, and rural rehabilitation. However, the program was an ambitious undertaking and was often wracked with corruption, in addition to the fact that it did not always reach the disenfranchised populations that needed help most. When Dunnigan questioned local WPA administrators, she discovered that some white women in Russellville pressured the WPA not to employ African-American women for fear that the substantial wage African-American women received from the WPA would spoil their own wage scale working as cooks in kitchens, thus denying white women any domestic help. Whether credited to her journalism experience in seeking answers or her natural talent for rising above adversity, Dunnigan attempted to form a civic league to gain a minimum wage for African-American cooks, and the WPA began hiring African-American women in Russellville. The episode typecast her as a troublemaker by both whites and blacks and did nothing to help her gain employment in her hometown.

Alice began to realize the only life available to her in Russellville was a life of indentured cleaning, washing, and teaching with meager pay. So she became the first African American to pass the Logan County civil service exam. In 1942 she took a typist job for the US War Labor Board in Washington, D.C., and left her son in the care of her parents. Earning twice her teaching salary, she attended night school at Howard University and was promoted to economist for the Office of Price Administration.

Although the position afforded her a phenomenal salary of $2,600 (twice that of the average African-American woman in Washington), Alice yearned for reaching her journalism apex. She began writing part-time for the Associated Negro Press (ANP). The Associated Negro Press was a Chicago-based news agency that supplied African-American newspapers around the country up-to-date news feed in the same manner as its mainstream presses. When ANP editor Claude Barnett needed a full-time Washington correspondent in 1947, he offered Alice the position at a salary $150 a week less than her male colleagues (who had incidentally turned him down). Barnett was unconvinced a women could handle the rigors of Washington. As a result, Dunnigan had to purchase her own typewriter, paper, notebooks, envelopes, and stamps all the while working sixteen-hour days, seven days a week.

Although blacks had fought alongside whites during World War II, they were still fighting for equal employment back in the states. Alice may have been in a war to overcome the wage and gender discrimination typical of the times, but her ascent into the journalism stratosphere was timed perfectly with the start of desegregation in American journalism. Eager to cover activity at the US Capitol, Dunnigan attempted to enter the Senate Press Gallery but discovered all the required press tools, such as typewriters, were reserved for accredited Capitol reporters. No African-American journalist was accredited.

Her first assignment called for her to cover the ousting of Theodore Bilbo of Mississippi from the US Senate. Since the Senate Press Gallery forbade black reporters, Alice had to cover her story standing alongside tourists peering down onto the US Senate floor. After the Bilbo incident she applied for press credentials. Her application occurred at the same time as *Atlanta Daily World* correspondent Louis Lautier appealed before the Senate Committee on Rules and Administration to have his press credentials accredited. At the end of his hearing, the Rules Committee overturned the standing committee and accredited Lautier. On June 1, 1947, Dunnigan followed suit and became the first African-American woman accredited to cover the US Congress. Two months later she secured credentials to cover the White House, Supreme Court, and the State Department.

Although these credentials were important, Alice sought the professional respect that comes with experience and perseverance. Financially struggling, she paid for prints to be filed among the 112 Associated Negro Press outlets. When Barnett refused to pay the $1,000 fee for travel expenses covering Truman's western US campaign, Alice trimmed her expenses to the bone and paid her own way. During the Eisenhower administration, she was often asked to submit her questions beforehand, yet she refused since other reporters were not required to do the same. She had to sit with servants while covering Senator Robert A. Taft's funeral. Her story on a 1949 incident detailing eighteen New York state delegates of Truman's inauguration being refused registration at a New York hotel garnered national attention in the black press, but not within mainstream US newspapers.

Her writing began to shift from covering the cultural aspects of African-American social life toward conditions of political life and civil rights for blacks. In 1961 she was one of the first African Americans appointed to John Kennedy's New Frontiers Administration, his inaugural theme advocating dramatic change in the country. She was appointed educational consultant to the President's Committee on Equal Employment Opportunity (CEEO), which was established to review employment practices of the federal government in terms of race, make recommendations for improvement, and develop anti-discrimination rules government contractors should follow. Even after Kennedy was assassinated, Lyndon Johnson pressed forward with the affirmative action mandate. Dunnigan's responsibility was to highlight the goals and objectives of the committee through press outlets, including news stories, speeches, and interviews. Between 1961 and 1965 Dunnigan made more than three hundred appearances as a representative of the committee.

Alice Dunnigan submitted reports to the president detailing not only conditions of African Americans across the United States but also black foreign visitors who served as official host delegates in Washington. By 1960 African Americans comprised 71 percent of the population of the city but were routinely denied housing in the city's choicest neighborhoods and apartment buildings. African diplomats and their families who moved to Washington, D.C., found it nearly impossible to find housing near their embassies or in upscale neighborhoods. Foreign dignitaries and their staffs were often slighted in Washington's better restaurants and public businesses. The severity of the problem eventually made its way to the White House after black ambassadors, their staffs, and their families were regularly thrown out of restaurants on Route 40, the highway that connected Washington, D.C., and New York. The White House created a special committee to eliminate segregation in restaurants in Maryland along Route 40 and Dunnigan was assigned to cover the efforts.

She became a prolific reporter detailing the effects of the Jim Crow laws on black America. She wrote extensively on issues ranging from cross burnings to black families being sued in white Washington, D.C., neighborhoods. She was even investigated by the FBI for being a Communist after reporting a story of seven Martinsville, Virginia, black men awaiting execution for raping a white woman. Her efforts proved meritorious. In 1951 she was awarded the Newsman's Trophy as the best African-American reporter in Washington and the Capital Press Club Best All-Around Newsman for 1951. She was awarded honorary degrees from the Normal and Industrial Institute, West Kentucky College, Louisville Municipal College, Tennessee A & I, and Howard University and an honorary doctorate from Colorado State College (1962). She was inducted into the University of Kentucky Journalism Hall of Fame (1982) and was the first black elected to the Women's National Press Club.

By the time Republicans returned to the White House, Alice retired and began writing her memoir, *A Black Woman's Experience: From Schoolhouse to White House,* published in 1974. Although she chronicled a lonely ascent to the top of journalism, she has been hailed as an inspiration for many promising minority journalists since her death of abdominal disease in 1983 at age seventy-seven. Her Russellville family members followed her fame in Washington and keep her spirit alive through museum exhibits and performances. One poignant reminder of Dunnigan's contributions to journalism occurred at the state capitol on March 6, 2007, when hundreds of family, friends, and elected officials crowded into the Frankfort rotunda to posthumously honor Dunnigan as a Kentucky Women Remembered (KWR) recipient. Dunnigan shares this distinguished honor with outstanding Kentucky women with backgrounds in law, the military, politics, medicine, and engineering.

Katherine Graham Peden

(1926–2006)

FIRST FEMALE STATE COMMERCE COMMISSIONER; ONLY WOMAN TO SERVE ON THE KERNER COMMISSION

While touring a housing project targeted by rioters in Newark, New Jersey, Katherine Peden walked alongside United Steelworkers president I. W. Abel, who suggested the National Advisory Committee on Civil Disorder organize some kids to clean up scattered trash. Instead, the kids started throwing trash at one another. Abel summarized the experience by telling Peden, "It's not those who are bombing and burning we should be most worried about. It's the next generation. Those kids will be growing up and be in a worse situation than exists today" (Lyne 1992, 344).

On a similar fact-finding trip at the infamous Los Angeles Watts housing project, residents attributed the 1965 riots to lack of employment, educational opportunities, and poor housing. Peden relayed this story to a 1964 White House social luncheon that gathered the nation's leading community and social activists and was hosted by Lady Bird Johnson. The revelation that she and her committee members discovered as they toured was that Katherine Peden's tenure as the Kerner Commission's first and only female member opened her eyes to the nation's most pressing racial problems.

This episode typified the findings of the twelve-member NACD report, eventually known as the Kerner Commission. The commission concluded the nation was moving toward two societies, one black and one white, that were separate and unequal. Peden was tapped by

Katherine Peden was the Democratic candidate for the US Senate seat from Kentucky who spoke and introduced Senator Edmund Muskie, vice-presidential candidate, who spoke while visiting the University of Kentucky campus on October 29, 1968. The University of Kentucky Photographic Archives

President Lyndon B. Johnson to serve on the Kerner Commission to investigate the urban race riots sweeping the country during 1966–1967. In contrast to the earlier civil right laws that focused on segregation and discrimination, the Kerner Commission investigated the economic inequality between blacks and whites, which the commission concluded was the result of inadequate employment and housing opportunities. Moreover, the commission members reported frustration of political and economic power among blacks fueled the belief that the country had steered in separate, unequal paths.

Peden and her eleven colleagues recommended that the Johnson administration focus initiatives in four areas: jobs, housing, education, and welfare. Suspicious of the committee criticism of him, President Johnson declined to endorse the findings. Nonetheless, the Kerner Commission spurred landmark legislation in open housing and an increase in federal housing, which produced 1.6 million units between 1970 and 1973. Low-income federally subsidized housing prevailed as a result of the commission's report well into the 1980s. The commission's assertion for two million jobs over a three-year period stimulated 750,000 jobs through public employment programs, including the Public Service Employment of the Comprehensive Employment and Training Act (CETA). The report further advocated expansion of spending to urban schools, remedial and adult education, and welfare, but these initiatives were eventually shuttered by the Reagan administration.

Never quite sure why Lyndon Johnson chose her, Katherine Graham Peden's national limelight overshadowed a self-assurance few would come up against. Born in Hopkinsville in 1926, Katherine was the daughter of a schoolteacher and construction superintendent. Voted most likely to succeed by her high school, Katherine established herself as class president, national honor society member, and debater whose peers included future Kentucky governor Edward Breathitt. She won a scholarship to the University of Louisville School of Pharmacy. She took a summer job at her local radio station, WHOP, making $18 a week to earn money for college. However, she enjoyed the broadcasting business and decided to scrap her plans for becoming a pharmacist. "I'd rather solve problems than mend headaches," Peden remarked in a 1961 *Washington Post* and *Times Herald* interview (Katherine Peden 1962).

Over the course of thirteen years, Peden worked her way up through the traffic department, as control room operator, announcer, and eventually program director. She told a *Billboard* magazine reporter that going to work in radio programming or sales was similar to professing wedding vows: "I take thee, radio, to be my working life, for better or for worse"("Says Better Logging Means Added Sales" 1952, 16). She eventually served as national sales manager for five CBS broadcasting stations, readily professing to broadcasters that they should start producing their own programs rather than wait for large sponsors to dictate programming. Opting out of a pharmacy license, she earned her engineer license with the Federal Communications Commission.

When she started working for WHOP in 1944, she also joined the local chapter of the National Federation of Business and Professional Women's Club (BPW), an early forerunner to the National Organization of Women. BPW was a nonprofit worldwide organization with the largest membership of business and professional women at the time. Cultivating business, scientific, and vocational activities at local, state, and national levels, BPW witnessed a steady increase in its membership, which included 175,000 women among the fifty states. BPW was instrumental in propelling the Equal Rights Amendment into legislation. Having successively served as president of the local Hopkinsville chapter, Peden moved up its ranks in the state chapter as its first vice president.

She became the youngest president in BPW's forty-three-year history when she held the post from 1961 to 1962. Accepting her post, Peden remarked to BPW annual conventioneers, "You will receive all I have to offer in leadership, in planning, in carrying out these directives"

("Katherine Peden" 1962). With these words, Peden initiated sweeping initiatives for the organization including a program to train women in executive and managerial positions, cooperative efforts with universities, and raising $10,000 to build a nurse's home in Formosa. Kentucky experienced the largest membership increase among all states within the BPW during Peden's presidency.

Traversing almost every state in the union, Peden embarked on a sweeping thirty-five-thousand-mile trip to twelve countries in Africa and the Middle East during her presidency. Her background in radio allowed her to interview individuals who promoted the BPW agenda. She represented the BPW United States delegation to the Conference of Business and Professional Women of the Americas, hoping to extend cultural, social, and economic partnership between women of North and South America. Her stature within a prominent national organization prompted then Kentucky governor Bert Combs to appoint her, the only woman, to a five-member personnel board to establish and administer Kentucky's first merit system for state employees in 1960. She resigned in 1962 to be the state chairwomen of primary and general elections, gaining ground in state politics.

Certainly her meteoric rise through BPW caught the eye of President John F. Kennedy, who approached her to serve on the Commission on the Status of Women. The commission handed their report to JFK one month before his assassination, citing widespread sex discrimination in the workplace, law, and adequate child care. The commission recommended Congress pass a law guaranteeing that women receive equal pay with men for equal duties performed. The passage of the Equal Pay Act of 1963 made it illegal for employers to pay female employees less for doing the same work as men. The passage of the nation's first women's civil rights legislation gave Peden satisfaction that her committee work provided the basis for breaking down employment prejudices of her time.

Peden's position as state chairwoman strengthened her interest in politics. Her former high school debate team member, Ed Breathitt, tapped her to run his campaign for governorship in 1962. The success of her campaign leadership prompted an unexpected phone call from Governor-elect Ed Breathitt to have Peden join his administration as the state's first female commerce commissioner. She replied to Breathitt, "You want me to do *what?*"(Lyne 1992, 336) Kentucky was having problems with a 6.9 percent unemployment rate, steady brain drain of educated Kentuckians, and a rising poverty rate. The proposition piqued her interest and raised a few eyebrows given that no woman had ever been elected to head a state development agency. Katherine knew the task would be challenging since one of Breathitt's campaign promises was to create seventy-five thousand new jobs in the state with no tax increases. This would mean she'd have to produce fifty new jobs a day, seven days a week for four years. However, the challenge was alluring since selling a state to prospective businesses was as intangible as selling radio advertising.

Boldly venturing where no woman had ventured before, Peden made swift changes to the agency starting with her office (painting it tangerine orange). She reorganized the agency without laying off staff and keeping politics out of the agency. Another innovation was a series of clinics to coach local organizations on the particulars of industrial development. She instituted community development ombudsmen to visit the state's leading companies twice a year to help service any problems. She was especially proud of her work rebuilding a stripped-out mining area of western Kentucky into an industrial park and Job Corp training center. This endeavor may have spurred the state legislature to enact a 1966 stringent law controlling strip mining.

Peden believed her femininity offered her a foot in the door since corporate America was curious to see what a female commerce commissioner looked like. She told a male reporter, "I had a big advantage over you men. Those prospects were awfully curious to see what a woman commissioner looked like" (Lyne 1992, 336). More importantly, she impressed her prospects by her sales and persuasion skills. She even impressed Kentucky citizens. Kentucky voters approved a $176 million revenue bond to accelerate building programs for roads, schools, and state parks. This feat even lured 125 local industrial foundations to sell $264 million worth of industrial revenue bonds to finance new plants or expansions in 1967.

Coined "Pedenblitz," Katherine embarked on a mission to win over business prospects with the state's largess. She commissioned a study to research the cost data on sixty-five state industries and four hundred related products for each of the sixteen Kentucky regions. Over a six-month period, her agency contacted approximately 13,000 CEOs from 888 companies with an introductory letter from the governor with his personal number. Several days later the agency followed up with a letter including a twelve-page analysis comparing the cost of the company doing business in Kentucky versus other established production centers. Interested parties were then contacted by the agency and subsequent meetings were held. Dubbed the "Katie Korps," the state opened offices in New York, Chicago, and Los Angeles in order to follow through with hot leads. Her role was so important that Breathitt had a special phone by his desk specifically designated to take calls only from the commerce commissioner.

Pedenblitz successfully lured American Electric Power Company and West Virginia Pulp & Paper to invest in the state. Donald Cook, then president of American Electric Power Company, considered Peden the most dynamic person in the field of industrial development. He noted that after a New York luncheon with Peden, he returned to his office and asked himself, "What can we do for Kentucky and do it now?" (Lyne 1992, 338). Within a few weeks the company earmarked three years' expenditure into one year. AEP subsidiary Kentucky Power Company eventually quadrupled its size of its Big Sandy generating unit, doubling the company's investment in the state. Ford Motor Company invested $85 million to $100 million on a 2.3-million-square-foot truck assembly plant in Louisville. West Virginia Pulp & Paper Company built an $80 million pulp and paper mill.

Peden's efforts paid off. By 1967 new non-farm jobs grew from 138,000 to 150,000; manufacturing jobs increased from 189,000 to 220,000. State unemployment dropped from 6.9 percent to 4.3 percent, despite General Electric layoffs in its Louisville appliance plant. Capital spending reached $1.25 billion compared to $405 million in the previous four years. Personal income reached 29 percent in the first three years and no taxes were increased. This success reverberated well into the 1990s when *Site Selection* magazine reported Kentucky finished sixth in the United States for new and expanded corporate facilities.

By the time her commerce term ended, Peden eyed higher political aspirations. A lifelong Democrat, Peden's grandfather served in the Kentucky Senate in the early 1900s. Once Peden put her hat in the ring for Kentucky's US Senate seat in 1968, State Senator Julian Carroll withdrew from the race. Peden was one of the most aggressive women leaders in public service. She easily defeated former Congressman John Y. Brown—his seventh try for the US Senate seat—in Kentucky's 1968 state primary. She turned her attention to beating Republican Marlow Cook by proclaiming herself an advocate of law and order in contrast to her opponent's proclamation that urban unrest is the work of Communists. Her initial campaign tactic was to highlight her role as the only female on the Kerner Commission; however, she found this strategy ultimately harmed her given that the report elicited unfavorable findings.

Although she carried 109 of the state's 120 counties, she fell short of victory by thirty thousand votes. Her loss may have been hampered not only by the Democratic state party refusing to support her financially, but her refusal to tap wealthy Democrat voters for fear she would lose voting autonomy while repaying party patronage. She told a reporter, "I knew good and well that if I took their money, I would never be my own person. Every time a vote came up one of them would be on the phone holding that contribution over my head" (Lyne 1992, 342). She failed to align with Hubert Humphrey, knowing that he boded poorly among Kentucky voters. Her Senate defeat ended any further political prospects and sidelined her with a debt that took her ten years to pay off.

Undeterred, Katherine embarked on a solo career, opening her own industrial and community development brokerage in 1973. Her firm, Peden and Associates, specialized in industrial and community development. The firm was successful in developing three business parks in Shelby County by utilizing a strong networking base among real estate and business prospects. She successfully lured Budd Company's $100 million auto-parts manufacturing plant and Reynolds Aluminum's Midwest distribution center. Tapping into her extensive network of site selection professionals, Peden took advantage of networking among real estate organizations. Adding to her accolades, she became the first woman to hold the Industrial Development Research Council's "master professional" title in 1983.

Given Kentucky's location, researchers have noted that the state has been dogged by the Appalachian region's slow economic development. Poorly developed social services, lack of economic opportunities, and high rates of poverty are factors as tall and wide as the rugged mountains that rule the Appalachian region. One of the most important studies Peden took part in was the Appalachian Land Ownership Task Force (ALOTF), which explored causes for the region's economic isolationism. The 1974 study concluded the region suffered from high levels of absentee landownership—as high as 94 percent—whose ownership was large but buffered by low taxes, large tracts of land, and limited diversification. Peden reported that the region's out-of-state ownership correlates with lower levels of manufacturing. Moreover, the coal industry, so prevalent in the region, exhibits high fluctuations in demand for housing, which in turn never materialize into economic growth opportunities. She voiced her concern: "You can spend all the money you want on trade shows, but if the community doesn't have things like water and sewer infrastructure and quality educational system, then you might as well forget it" (Lyne 1992, 339).

Along with her appointment to President Jimmy Carter's 1978 Executive Committee of the White House Conference on Balanced Growth and Economic Development, Katherine Peden was often solicited by Kentucky's successive governors for input on the state's economic development strategy. She advocated incentives essential for helping both communities and corporations balance unfavorable economic conditions. Financial incentives used for business relocation prospects included tax concessions, revenue bonds, statewide development credit corporations, and loan guarantees. Many of these financial incentives were originally created for small or medium-size firms looking to locate in urban perimeters but lacking investment capital. By the mid- to late 1960s, many larger corporations took advantage of these financial incentives.

Many experts contend that financial incentives are not the primary factor for business relocation prospects but other factors play a larger role (i.e., labor, markets, and transportation). Peden's 1974 study cautioned that state subsidization programs should avoid eroding the tax base and maintain, if not exceed, income needed for public services. "The thing you've got to remember about incentives," Peden told a reporter, "is that if a company wants you to provide the building and land and buy their equipment, they can move out as fast as they move in" (Lyne 1992, 340).

Her role in economic development prompted Peden to serve on the Kentucky Environmental Quality Commission and the Louisville-Jefferson County Air Board. Although she never labeled herself an environmentalist, Peden realized taxpayers, local communities, and state government were cash strapped. Peden was often approached by Kentucky governors as an unofficial advisor in state economic development. She served as a director for Westvaco Corporation, MidAmerica Bancorp, Bank of Louisville, and Norfolk-Southern Corporation. She refuted being labeled a lobbyist, preferring instead to be considered a "sounding board" for companies on issues and state affairs. Even in her retirement years, Peden volunteered and hosted state civic and educational groups. One example included her coordination of joint ventures between a University of Kentucky study group with the northern European cities of Warsaw and Prague in the coal industry.

Although she never married, Peden maintained an active life, traveling to as many as one hundred countries, especially during her tenure in state and national positions. In the same manner as her intense research for economic development, Peden thoroughly investigated each trip on which she embarked. She played a mean round of golf, highlighted by a handicap of nine during her pre-Commerce Department tenure. Mindful of the role basketball played in the state's psyche, Peden rooted for both University of Kentucky and University of Louisville basketball teams. She was a regular attendee of racing at Churchill Downs. Later in life she felt there were still personal adventures to see and do. She told a reporter in 1992, "And one more thing I want to do concerns the Brandenburg Gate. I've seen it from the west side, and I've seen it from the east side. Now I want to walk *through* it" (Lyne 1992, 346). In 2006 Peden quietly walked through another set of doors when she passed away after a long illness. No doubt Kentucky's preeminent saleswoman will not be forgotten.

BIBLIOGRAPHY

Jane Coomes

Chinn, George Morgan. *Kentucky Settlement and Statehood 1750-1800.* Frankfort: The Kentucky Historical Society, 1975.

Clark, Thomas D. *A History of Kentucky.* New York: Prentice Hall, 1937.

———. "Education." *Our Kentucky: A Study of the Bluegrass State.* Lexington: University Press of Kentucky, 2000.

Harrington, F. C. *Kentucky: A Guide to the Bluegrass State.* New York: Harcourt, Brace & Company, 1939.

Perrin, W. H., J. H. Battle, and G. C. Kniffin. *Kentucky: A History of the State.* Louisville, KY: F.A. Battey and Company, 1887.

"Site of dedication honoring first teacher in the state: illustrations." *The Record.* 27 Feb. 1936: 47.

Walker, Michael. "Frances Jane Greenleaf." Nov. 30, 2004. http://familytreemaker.genealogy.com/users/w/a/l/Mike-J-Walker/WEBSITE-0001/UHP-0051.html

Webb, Benedict. *Catholic Emigration to Kentucky: The Centenary of Catholicity of Kentucky.* Louisville, KY: J.C. Webb Company, 1884.

Catherine Spalding

Doyle, Mary Ellen, SCN. *Pioneer Spirit: Catherine Spalding, Sister of Charity of Nazareth.* Lexington, KY: The University Press of Kentucky, 2006.

Harrington, F. C. *Kentucky: A Guide to the Bluegrass State.* New York: Harcourt, Brace & Company, 1939.

Harrison, Lowell H. and James C. Klotter. *New History of Kentucky.* Lexington: The University Press of Kentucky, 1997.

Kentucky Bicentennial Commission. *The Kentucky Encyclopedia.* Lexington: The University Press of Kentucky, 1992.

McGann, Agnes G. *Nativism in Kentucky in 1860.* Washington, DC: Catholic University of America, 1944.

McGill, Anna B. *The Sisters of Charity of Nazareth.* New York: The Encyclopedia Press, 1917.

Margaret Garner

Coffin, Levi. *Reminiscences of Levi Coffin.* New York: Arno Press, 1898.

Gilmore, M. T. "Margaret Garner: A Cincinnati Story" in Christoph K. Lohmann's *Discovering Difference: Contemporary Essays in American Culture.* Bloomington: Indiana University Press, 1993, 112–119.

Morrison, Jago. *Contemporary Fiction.* New York: Taylor & Francis, 2003.

Taylor, Nikki Marie. *Frontiers of Freedom: Cincinnati's Black Community, 1802-1868.* Athens: Ohio University Press, 2004.
Weisenburger, Steven. *Modern Medea: A Family Story of Slavery and Child-Murder from the Old South.* New York: Hill and Wang, 1998.
Yanuck, Julius. "The Garner Fugitive Slave Case." Mississippi Valley Historical Review (June 1953), 1–20.

Julia Marcum

Kentucky Historical Society. "Julia A. Marcum" (Aug. 7, 1926), Nov. 21, 2008, http://freepages.history.rootsweb.ancestry.com/~honeycutt/juliaannmarcum.html.
"Kentucky's Only Woman Soldier." *Louisville Courier Journal,* June 2, 1940.
Klebenow, Anne. *200 Years through 200 Stories: A Tennessee Bicentennial Collection.* Knoxville: University of Tennessee, 1996.
McKnight, Brian D. *Contested Borderland: The Civil War in Appalachian Kentucky and Virginia.* Lexington: The University Press of Kentucky, 2006.
Reports of Committees: 48th Congress, Second session. February 20, 1885. United States. Congress. Senate. HR 5938.
Stith, Matthew M. "Sister States, Enemy States: The Civil War in Kentucky and Tennessee." *Arkansas Review: A Journal of Delta Studies, vol.* 41, no. 1 (April 2010): 72. *MasterFILE Premier,* EBSCO*host.* Accessed via Internet on March 24, 2011.
West, Timothy N. *Scott County, Tennessee History.* (Sept. 6, 2008) Nov. 21, 2008, http://www.tngenweb.org/scott.

E. Belle Mitchell

Byars, Laura F. *Lexington's Colored Orphan Industrial Home: Building for the Future.* Lexington: I.B. Bold Publications, 1995.
Hogan, Roseann R., Ph.D. African American Research, Part 3: Case Studies, www.ancestrymagazine.com/1996/11/ancestry-magazine/african-american-research-part-3-case-studies/.
Sears, Richard. *A Utopian Experiment in Kentucky: Integration and Social Equality at Berea, 1866-1904.* Westport, CT: Greenwood Press, 1996.
———. *Camp Nelson, Kentucky: A Civil War History.* Lexington: The University of Kentucky Press, 2002.
Williams, Heather Ann. *Self-Taught: African American Education in Slavery and Freedom.* Chapel Hill: The University of North Carolina Press, 2005.

Captain Mary Garretson Miller

"Capt. Mary M. Miller Licensed." *New York Times,* 19 Februrary 1884: 1.
Curry, Jane. *The River's in My Blood: Riverboat Pilots Tell Their Story.* Lincoln, NE: University of Nebraska Press, 1983.

Custer, Jack E. and Sandra Miller Custer. "Mary Millicent Miller." Kleber, John E. *The Encyclopedia of Louisville.* Lexington: The University Press of Kentucky, 2000, 621.

Eskew, G. L. 1929. "Father of the Steamboat." *Popular Mechanics* 52, no. 3: 442–447.

"First Woman Steamboat Master." *New York Times,* 6 November 1894: 1.

Gordon, Ann D., ed. 2006. *The Selected Papers of Elizabeth Cady Stanton and Susan B. Anthony: When Clowns Make Laws for Queens 1880 to 1887.* Piscataway, NJ: Rutgers, the State University of New Jersey.

Hall, Henry. *Report on the Ship-building Industry of the United States.* Washington, DC: Government Printing Office, 1884.

"Her Claim Not Recognized: A Woman Who Wanted a License as a Steam-boat Captain." *New York Times,* 7 December 1883: 1.

Putnam, G. P. *Ten Years of the World's Progress.* New York: G.P. Putnam, 1861.

Enid Yandell

"Americans Aid French Artists." *New York Times,* 30 May 1915: 2.

Baird, Nancy D. "Enid Yandell: Kentucky Sculptor." *The Filson Club Quarterly* (January, 1988), 5–31.

Crowe-Carraco, Carol. "Enid Yandell" in Carol Crowe-Carraco's *Women Who Made a Difference.* Lexington, KY: University Press of Kentucky, 1989. 29–34.

Ladegast, Richard. "Enid Yandell, the Sculptor." *The Outlook* (January–April 1902), 81–83.

Loughborough, Jean, Laura Hayes, and Enid Yandell. "Our Holiday" in Jean Loughborough, Laura Hayes, and Enid Yandell's *Three Girls in a Flat.* Chicago: Leonard Knight & Co., 1892, 103.

Sangha, Soni. "Landowner Scolded for Removing Sculpture; Nearby Couple Issue Plea for Missing Cow." *The Bergen County Record,* Feb. 1 2006: 2.

Taft, Loredo. *The History of American Sculpture.* New York: The MacMillan Company, 1903.

Patty Smith Hill

"Happy Birthday, We'll Sue." Snopes.com. www.snopes.com/music/songs/birthday .asp. Accessed April 10, 2010.

"Hill, Patty Smith." *New World Encyclopedia.* www.newworldencyclopedia.org/entry/ Patty_Smith_Hill. Accessed April 10, 2010.

"History of the Birthday Song." Tokenz.com. www.tokenz.com/history-of-birthday-song.html. Accessed April 10, 2010.

Jammer, M. Charlotte. *Patty Smith Hill and Reform of the American Kindergarten.* New York: Teachers College, Columbia University, 1960.

Lichtman, Irv. "Most-Performed Song of the Century." *Billboard,* Jan. 8, 2000, 109.

Nash, Paul. "Froebel, Friedrich Wilhelm August." *Grolier Multimedia Encyclopedia.* Grolier Online http://gme.grolier.com/article?assetid=0113410-0. Accessed March 28, 2011.

Ross, Elizabeth D. "Patty Smith Hill." *Dictionary of American Biography, Supplement 4: 1946-1950.* Washington, D.C.: American Council of Learned Societies, 1974.

Rudnitski, Rose A. 1995. "Patty Smith Hill, gifted early childhood educator of the progressive era." *Roeper Review* 18, no. 1: 19. *Academic Search Premier,* EBSCO*host* (accessed May 1, 2011).

Wollons, Roberta, L. *Kindergartens and Cultures: The Global Diffusion of an Idea.* New Haven, CT: Yale University Press, 2000.

Sophonisba Breckinridge

*Chicago School of Civics & Philanthropy: Bulletin.*July, 1909 1 (1):15-20.

Fitzpatrick, Ellen. *Endless Crusade: Women Social Scientists and Progressive Reform.* Cary, NC: Oxford University Press, 1994.

Hammond, Claire Holton. "Sophonisba Breckinridge (1866-1948)" in Robert W. Dimand, Mary Ann Dimand and Evelyn L. Forget's *A Biographical Dictionary of Women Economists.* Cheltenham Press: Edward Elgar Publishing, 2000, 81–87.

Johnson, Joan M. *Southern Women at the Seven Sister Colleges.* Athens: University of Georgia Press, 2008.

Muncy, Robyn. *Creating a Female Dominion in American Reform, 1890-1935.* Cary, NC: Oxford University Press, 1994.

Toft, Jessica and Laura S. Abrams. "Progressive Maternalists and the Citizenship Status of Low-Income Single Mothers." *Social Service Review* (September 2004): 447–465.

Nannie Helen Burroughs

"Burroughs, Nannie." Grolier Multimedia Encyclopedia. Grolier Online, 2011, http://gme.grolier.com/article?assetid=0046810-0. Accessed March 14, 2011.

Hammond, L. H. *In the Vanguard of a Race.* New York: Council of Women for Home Missions and Missionary Education Movement of the United States and Canada, 1922.

Harley, Sharon. "Nannie Helen Burroughs: The Black Goddess of Liberty." *The Journal of Negro History* (Annual 1996): 62–72

Taylor, Traki L. "Womanhood Glorified: Nannie Helen Burroughs and the National Training School for Women and Girls, Inc., 1909-1961." *The Journal of African American History* (Fall 2002): 390–403.

Wolcott, Victoria W. "Bible, Bath, and Broom: Nannie Helen Burroughs's Training School and African American Racial Uplift." *Journal of Women's History* (Spring 1997): 388–411.

Laura Clay

Breckinridge, Madeline. "Kentucky" in Ida Harper et al. *The History of Woman Suffrage.* New York: Source Book Press, 1970. 207–215.

James, Edward, Janet W. James, and Paul Boyer. *Notable American Women: A Biographical Dictionary.* Boston: Harvard University Press, 1971.

Johnson, Kenneth R. "White Racial Attitudes as a Factor in the Arguments against the Nineteenth Amendment." *Phylon* (1970): 31–37.

"'Leaders Cannot Win,' Says Palmer Just Before Night Session Begins." *New York Times,* July 6, 1920: 1–2.

Wheeler, Marjorie S. *New Women of the New South: The Leaders of the Woman Suffrage Movement in the Southern States.* Cary, NC: Oxford University Press, 1993.

———. *Votes for Women!: The Suffrage Movement in Tennessee, the South, and the Nation.* Knoxville: The University of Tennessee Press, 1995.

Mary Breckinridge

"A tradition of service: Midwifery school builds on founder's legacy." *Lexington Herald-Leader* (Lexington, KY) (June 25, 2007): NA. General OneFile. Gale. March 31, 2011. http://find.galegroup.com/gtx/start.do?prodId=ITOF&userGroupName=lfpl.

Barney, Sandra. *Authorized to Heal: Gender, Class, and the Transformation of Medicine in Appalachia, 1880-1930.* Chapel Hill, NC: The University of North Carolina Press, 2000.

Bartlett, Marie. "Frontier nursing service." *Grit* Feb. 2005: 12. General OneFile. March 31, 2011. http://find.galegroup.com/gtx/infomark.do?&contentSet=IAC-Documents&type=retrieve&tabID=T003&prodId=ITOF&docId=A130468908&source=gale&srcprod=ITOF&userGroupName=lfpl&version=1.0.

Breckinridge, Mary. *Wide Neighborhoods: A Story of the Frontier Nursing Service.* Lexington: The University Press of Kentucky, 1952.

Goan, Melanie Beals. *Mary Breckinridge: The Frontier Nursing Service and Rural Health in Appalachia.* Chapel Hill: The University of North Carolina Press, 2008.

"Mary Breckinridge." *World of Health* online. Thomson Gale, 2006. Reproduced in *Biography Resource Center.* Farmington Hills, MI: Gale, 2009. http://galenet.galegroup.com/servlet/BioRC.

Rooks, Judith. *Midwifery and Childbirth in America.* Philadelphia: Temple University Press, 1997.

Aunt Molly Jackson

"Aunt Molly Jackson, 80, Dead; Original 'Pistol Packin' Mama.'" *New York Times,* September 3, 1960, page 17.

Hevener, John W. *Which Side Are You On?: The Harlan County Coal Miners, 1931-39.* Urbana-Champaign: University of Illinois Press, 2002.

Lynch, Timothy. *Strike Songs of the Depression.* Jackson, MS: University Press of Mississippi, 2001.

Martin, Darcy. "Aunt Molly Jackson: The Perfect Miner's Voice (Romalis 3). *Journal of American & Comparative Cultures* 25(3-4): 468–78. 2002.

Reuss, Richard, and Joanne Reuss. *American Folk Music and Left-Wing Politics, 1927-1957.* Lanham, MD: Scarecrow Press, 2000.

Romalis, Shelly. *Pistol Packin' Mama: Aunt Molly Jackson and the Politics of Folksong.* Urbana-Champaign: University of Illinois Press, 1998.

Wald, Alan. *The New York Intellectuals: The Rise and Decline of the Anti-Stalinist Left from the 1930s to the 1980s.* Chapel Hill: The University of Carolina Press, 1987.

Yurchenco, Henrietta. "Trouble in the Mines: A History in Song and Story by Women of Appalachia," *American Music* (Summer, 1991), Vol. 9, No. 2, 209–224.

Laura Miller Derry

Derry, Laura M. "How the Court Martial System Works and Suggestion to Improve," in *Women Lawyers Journal,* Vol. 32, No. 3, September, 1946.

———. *The Digest of Women Lawyers and Judges,* Louisville, Kentucky: Dunne Press, c. 1949.

Morden, Bettie J. *Women's Army Corps, 1945-1978.* Washington, DC: U.S. Government Printing Office, 1990.

Porter, Marion. "Woman Attorney Defends Soldier in Fort Knox Rape Trial—and Wins," *Louisville Courier Journal,* November 19, 1944.

Smith, Selma. "A Century of Achievement: The Centennial of the National Association of Women Lawyers," in *Experience Magazine,* Vol. 9, Issue 1, Fall 1998.

Turner, Lisa L. "The Articles of War and the UMCJ," in *Aerospace Power Journal,* Fall, 2000. http://findarticles.com/p/articles/mi_m0ICK/is_3_14/ai_68507686. Accessed on March 21, 2005.

Alice Allison Dunnigan

"Alice Allison Dunnigan." *Encyclopedia of World Biography Supplement,* Vol. 25 (2005): Biography Resource Center. http://galenet.galegroup.com. Gale. Accessed Apr. 10, 2010.

Crowe-Carraco, Carol. *Women Who Made a Difference.* Lexington: The University Press of Kentucky, 1989.

Dawson, Nancy J. "Alice Allison Dunnigan: Led the Fight for Black Journalists." *Crisis* (15591573) 114, no. 4 (July 2007): 39-41. Academic Search premier, EBSCO*host.* Accessed April 1, 2010.

"More About the WPA." www.indiana.edu/~liblilly/wpa/wpa_info.html. Accessed March 29, 2011.

O'Brien, Michael. *John F. Kennedy: A Biography.* New York: St. Martin's Press, 2005.

Romano, Renee. "No Diplomatic Immunity: African diplomats, the State Department, and Civil Rights, 1961-1964." *The Journal of American History* 87(2) (September, 2000): 546–579, doi: 2307/2568763.

Streitmatter, Rodger. *Raising Her Voice: African American Women Journalists Who Changed History.* Lexington: The University Press of Kentucky, 1994.

Katherine Graham Peden

Applebome, Peter. "From Riots of '60s to Riots of the '90s, a Frustrating Search to Heal a Nation." *New York Times* (May 8, 1992): A19.

Goodstein, Eban. "Landownership, Development, and Poverty in Southern Appalachia." *The Journal of Developing Areas* (July 1989): 519-534.

"How Katie Makes Kentucky Grow." *Business Week* (September 1967): 184–190.

"Katherine Peden." *Current Biography.* The H.W. Wilson Company, May 1962. 28–30.

Lyne, Jack. "Peden & Associates' Katherine Peden: A Woman Who Opened Closed Doors." *Site Selection & Industrial Development* (April 1992): 336–340.

Richardson, Darcy. *A Nation Divided: The 1968 Presidential Campaign.* Lincoln, NE: iUniverse.com (2002).

"Says Better Logging Means Added Sales." *Billboard Magazine* (May 17, 1952): 16.

"Today's America: Better or Worse? Decade of the Woman." *U.S. News & World Report* (1971): 30–31.

Verbrugge, James. "Incentives for Industrial Development." *Georgia Government Review* (Autumn, 1974): 4–8.

General Sources

Clark, Thomas D., PhD. *A History of Kentucky.* New York: Prentice Hall, 1937.

Kleber, John E. *The Encyclopedia of Louisville.* Lexington: University Press of Kentucky, 2001.

Kleber, John E., Lowell H. Harrison, and Thomas Dionysius Clark. *The Kentucky Encyclopedia.* Lexington: University Press of Kentucky, 1992.

INDEX

D

I

J

K

L

M

N

T

U

V

W

Y

ABOUT THE AUTHOR

Mimi O'Malley holds a bachelor's degree in history and communication arts from the University of Dayton and a master's in library science from Clarion University of Pennsylvania. She taught information literacy classes for four years at Jefferson Community and Technical College. The author currently works as a digital curriculum specialist at the Learning House.

O'Malley is the author of *It Happened in Kentucky* (Globe Pequot Press, 2006) and a contributor to three chapters of *It Happened in Georgia* (TwoDot Books, 2000). She has written for national, regional, and online publications including *CollegeBound Magazine, DECA Dimensions: The Publication of the Association for Marketing Students, Kentucky Libraries, LifeGlow Magazine, Teachers of Vision, Twin & Turbine Magazine, BusinessFirst Louisville, World War II Magazine,* Mom Online.com, Atthefence.com, *Naperville Press Publications, Batavia Press Publications, Kane County Chronicle,* and *ChicagoParent.*

Her specialties include history, biography, and nonfiction with an emphasis on unusual, eclectic, and little-known details. Her book *It Happened in Kentucky* has been considered for implementation in developmental reading classes and won appeal with non-native English language learners for its ability to capture Kentucky history in a quick storytelling fashion. She lives in Louisville, Kentucky, with her husband and two children.